Wicca *and* Astrology

How They Work Together

CHARLYN SCHEFFELMAN

(Lady Nytewind)

BALBOA.PRESS
A DIVISION OF HAY HOUSE

Balboa Press books may be ordered through booksellers or by contacting:

Balboa Press
A Division of Hay House
1663 Liberty Drive
Bloomington, IN 47403
www.balboapress.com
844-682-1282

Print information available on the last page.

ISBN: 978-1-9822-7730-7 (sc)
ISBN: 978-1-9822-7731-4 (e)

Balboa Press rev. date: 12/08/2021

CONTENTS

RITUALS

CHAPTER 1

WICCA AND ASTROLOGY

(HOW THEY WORK TOGETHER)
PART ONE – KNOW THYSELF

Moons and Meaning

The best means that I know of to accomplish this is through Astrology! There were three very important things happening when you were born; the astrological placement of the Sun, the Moon, and the Rising Sign; the sign and degree rising in the east all are determined by the longitude and latitude and exact time you were born. This information provides a map of the heavens and the energies present at your birth. This will give you tons of information about yourself, parents, abilities, weaknesses, etc. etc.

I look at it this way – imprinting!!! We know that when something (or one) is born into this world it is first imprinted with the knowledge of its mother. I believe that it is also imprinted by the energies of the planets, moon, etc. – all the energies that are present – as well! I guarantee you that any competent astrologer can accurately determine your talents, weaknesses, etc. by looking at your accurate birth chart!

The Moon

The Goddess has three different forms: the Maiden, the Mother, and the Crone (the old wise woman). Each phase of the moon is associated with a phase of the Goddess; the "new moon" is the maiden, the "full moon" is the mother, and the "dark moon" is the wise old crone.

As you might have suspected, if you are beginning a project, begin on a new moon for best results. If you are in the planning stages, use the wisdom of the Crone during the dark moon.

In an astrological chart, the moon equals the emotions. Some Gods associated with the moon are Morigu, Horus, Shiva, and some Moon Goddesses are Isis, Diana, and Luna. In Astrology, the moon represents home, houses, real estate, a parent, (usually the mother), and the subconscious mind. It is the fastest moving body in Astrology and changes signs every 2 ½ days. The moon has an effect on fluids, in the body and in nature.

Its Astrological sign is Cancer, the crab and it rules the emotional nature, moods, emotions and how you display them, the source of your emotional security, your shadow self, subconscious, and habits. It rules sleep, Insanity (lunatic), manias, psychic abilities, spiritualism, breasts, milk, fluids, caregivers, nurses, mothers, childbirth, the stomach, food, careers, kitchens, the public (especially women), water, the sea, rain, and more.

Associated with: Night blooming or white flowers, moonwort, chickweed, hyssop, willow, lotus, and water-growing plants

Metal – *Silver, aluminum*

Three Water Signs: The zodiac represents three qualities of each element; Fire, Air, Earth, Water, and Spirit. The moon represents the water signs:

Cancer – *warm, moving water (gentle waves)*

Scorpio – *Hot, seething water, water below the surface, similar to the geysers in Yellowstone Park.*

Pisces – *Deep, still water (ocean depths)*

The position of the moon on the day and time of your birth has a lot to do with your emotional makeup. It also reveals the relationship with your own mother.

Moons through the signs: your Birth Chart

Aries – probably mother's pet, spoiled by her. Not a good moon for a man, as he might resent women.

Taurus – Mother concerned for the child's welfare—overprotective and may be over-ambitious

Gemini – Versatile mother, busy with outside interests—maybe too busy for the child's good

Cancer – overprotective smother love, but takes good care of the children

Leo – Mother may have inadvertently encouraged vanity and pride

Virgo – not a warm mother, probably nagged. Child becomes self-conscious but easily picks up mother's prejudices

Libra – Mother may have fostered superficial behavior—too much concern over what other people think and say

Scorpio – Forceful about child's career and life choices, Can be a "stage mother" and probably has psychic talents

Sagittarius – Mother may have been more of a 'pal' than typical mother image

Capricorn – Mother may have had a hard time warming up to this child or was very ambitious for him/her.

Aquarius – eccentric mother, ahead of her times, very unusual, not particularly warm

Pisces – Easygoing permissive mother, child needed stronger direction.

Day – The moon rules Monday

Knowing your Sun sign and your Moon Sign will give you great information, but of course, you would know a lot more if you had your astrological chart. There are sites on the web that can calculate this for you if you know the exact time, date, and place of your birth. Knowing how many planets are in each elemental sign would be helpful, too. For instance, if you had most of your planets in fire and air signs, you would have trouble being practical and/or committed to mundane things. You'd be good at getting ideas and starting things up, but not always sticking to the task.

CHAPTER 2

THE ELEMENTS - ALSO OF GREAT IMPORTANCE

The Element of Air:

The elements play an enormous role in the natural Magick that Wiccans do. They are more than physical elements, more than what we see and feel. They are symbolic of physical, spiritual and emotional attributes.

Air symbolizes the mind and the conception or perception of new ideas, knowledge, creativity and self-expression. It is related to learning, invention and inspiration. It is the creator, for words have power—"in the beginning there was the word", or 'it is written as it is spoken'.

It is the element of new life, springtime, new possibilities and the magic of the four winds. Wishes and dreams, visualization and freedom are also associated with this element.

Direction: *East*
Color: *Yellow*
Time of Day: *Dawn*
Season: *Spring*

5

Elemental Spirits:	*Sylphs, Air Fairies and Zephyrs*
Animal creatures:	*Eagles, all birds and other winged creatures*
Archangel:	*Raphael*
Magickal Tool:	*Wand, athame, sword, incense*
Virtue:	*To know*
Herbs:	*Lavender, pine, almond and eyebright*
Stones Pumice:	*Amethyst, sapphire, citrine, mica, pumice*
Attributes:	*Vision, voice, free movement*
Astrological Sign:	*Aquarius, Gemini and Libra*
Elemental King:	*Paralda*
Other:	*Hermes or Mercury; Messenger of the Gods, and Thoth*
Symbol:	

Source: Carolyn White "A History of Irish Fairies"

The folklore beings are many, but the ones that hold the strongest position are the Gutnish fairies or "di sma undar jordi" in Gutnish. These fairies live in the ground and have a community just like humans. The main Gutnish folklore beings are the following:

In Gotland people have believed that the earth is inhibited by small beings, like the fairies and pixies of the Celtic countries. These people have been named "Di sma undar jordi", or only "Di sma" which means "The little ones under the earth", or just "The little ones". They were also called "Di undarboniske", which roughly means "The underliving".

They have been described in different ways, but often as having grey or blue clothes, with a cap on their head, and small as an infant.

Offerings

"In the grass on fields you can see rings from "Di sma", which have danced there. To cure certain illnesses that have suddenly started after you have laid on the ground, people normally lay a silver coin or a penny as an offering in the middle of the ring and then walk away without turning or looking for it again. Others usually pour out milk or linseeds, beer or salt in these rings. Some also do this to prevent getting sick." C. Lindgren, 19th century.

It was believed that simply by lying on the ground, you could disturb the little ones, and offerings were often made to appease them.

Protection against "Di sma"

There is a special plant that is known to cure diseases from "Di sma" as well as being protecting towards them; Tarald (Cucubalus Behen). Hainumkéllingi used to pick it on midsummers-eve. Against fairie-illnesses you should smoke tarald or wash with Garlic. Milk from a white goat could also be used.

Hainumkellingi

These beings could be dangerous if you treated them ill, but if you were good or helped them in any way it could be very rewarding. It was said that "Di sma" held great knowledge in curing diseases, and a wise woman - called Hainumkellingi living in the 18th century in the village of Hainum in Gotland - has testified that she was taken down into the ground to the land of "Di sma" and kept there for several days. While there, she learned how to cure diseases and was soon widely known for her abilities and knowledge of healing.

She also was taken to court and prosecuted for witchcraft. She served several months in prison for this charge. It was in court that she gave statements describing her travels to the underworld.

The world is full of "unseen" entities, but some of us do see them – perhaps you do. Departed human spirits, spirits of animals, dragons and fairies, angels, too; they all exist. After all, knowing that the Cern Hadron collider has opened up thirteen different dimensions (last I heard), anything could potentially be living anywhere!

The Element of Fire

Fire was a life or death matter to ancient people. It kept them alive in cold months and kept predatory animals at bay. It gave light and heat necessary to make tools and weapons of metal, and cook the meat and bread needed for nourishment. The fire of the sun warmed the Earth so plants could grow and all survive

It was the first magick, and a mystery as well. It came to earth in streaks of lightening sent directly from heaven; or sometimes from the depths of the earth in the form of burning rock. It could be a fearsome source of destruction, setting forests and grasslands ablaze, threatening all that man had built and planted. Its awesome power was highly revered by all ancient people, and there are many myths concerning the gifts of fire from the Gods.

The energy of Fire/South is strong. It represents the will, the desires and the passions of humankind. It can also be a strong protector—a warrior if you need one, a healer, or a destroyer of bad habits. It is the element of authority and leadership. It is used for purification, energy, and transformation.

Direction:	*South*
Color:	*Red*
Time of Day:	*Noon*
Season:	*Summer*
Elemental Spirits:	*Salamanders, firedrakes and dragon*
Animal:	*Lion*
Archangel:	*Michael*
Magickal Tool:	*Athame, sword, flames and thurible*
Virtue:	*To will*
Herbs:	*Blood root, Dragons Blood, Ginger, Yucca, Tobacco*
Stones:	*Ruby, Garnet, Bloodstone, Flint, Obsidian*
Attributes	*Passion, Lust, Will, Desire, Transformation*
Astrological Signs:	*Aries, Leo, and Sagittarius*
Symbol:	

The Element of Water

The element of Water represents the Goddess, especially her Mother aspect, as does the chalice, the cauldron and any other bowl that holds liquids. The Moon, which is also a symbol of the Goddess, acts on and affects the waters of earth and the liquids of our bodies directly.

Water is associated with birth and fertility. It is the source of life and the vital element for survival. It is also an element of mystery, able to transform itself from one state of matter to another—gas, liquid, or solid. It is in itself a cycle, falling from the sky only to eventually evaporate back into the sky to fall again. As such, it represents the cycle of birth, death, and rebirth. Many sacred places are found near water; ponds, lakes, rivers and streams, or sometimes bubbling hot directly from the earth, creating healing mineral springs.

Water is associated with feelings and emotions, intuition and divination. It is receptive and sensitive, the past and the future. Like our emotions, it can also be destructive—floods, hurricanes, violent storms and tidal waves remind us that water is a powerful element.

Direction	West
Color:	Blue
Time of Day:	Twilight
Season:	Autumn
Elemental Spirits:	Merfolk, Undines
Animal:	Serpent, Sea Creatures
Archangel:	Gabriel
Magickal Tool:	Chalice, cauldron, bowl
Virtue:	To Dare
Herbs:	Chamomile, Eucalyptus, Gardenia, Jasmine
Stones:	Blue agate, Coral, Crystals, Geodes, Jade, Sapphire
Attributes:	Feeling, reflection, receptivity
Astrological Signs:	Cancer, Scorpio, Pisces
Symbol:	▽

You can do a little analysis of yourself by just knowing what sign your Sun and Moon are in. There are several free sites on the internet where you can have your chart drawn. You need to know what <u>time</u> you were born as well as the month, day, and place of your birth. The horoscope is a picture of the placement of the sun, moon, and all the planets that surround the earth at that particular moment in time. Then you can also find out, for instance, how many planets were in fire signs, or perhaps in earth when you were born? What sign was coming up on the eastern horizon? All these things are relevant.

I highly suggest getting the correct time and place of your birth if you can so you can get an accurate birth chart. But even if you can't the signs of the sun, the number of planets in each element, and the moon, if it's not too close to moving into the next, can give you much information about yourself.

I high recommend getting as much of this information as you can.

The Element of Earth

The Earth is our Mother. She gives us life, she nourishes us and gives us a beautiful, varied home on which to live. She brings forth millions of kinds of animals and plant life; on and under the Earth and its waters. She brings fourth beautiful and useful minerals and gems.

But she is also powerful beyond measure. She has only to shrug, and the buildings of man tumble. She has only to belch and she emits poisonous gasses. She has only to vomit and the countryside is laid waste under tons of molten, burning lava or ash. She is, therefore, to be doubly revered, both for her life-giving fertility and her tremendous power.

Earth represents our physical bodies and our connections with the material world. From the element of Earth, we can obtain balance in our lives, abundance and prosperity, stability and wisdom. But we must always remember to take care of Mother Earth, to be as ecologically minded as we can be, and to return our energies to her through rituals and libations.

Direction:	*North*
Color:	*Green*
Time of Day:	*Midnight*
Season:	Winter
Elemental Spirits:	*Gnomes, Dwarves, Dryads*
Animal:	*Bull, Bear*
Archangel:	*Uriel*

Magickal Tool:	*Pentagram, salt, stones, soil*
Virtue:	*To keep silent*
Herbs	*Alfalfa, honeysuckle, mugwort, patchouli, sagebrush*
Stones:	*Moss agate, emerald, jet, malachite, tourmaline*
Attributes:	*Strength, patience, stability, balance, fertility, wisdom*
Astrological Sign:	*Taurus, Virgo, and Capricorn*
Symbol:	

CHA3TER

INTRODUCTION TO WICCA—
WHAT IT IS, AND WHAT IT ISN'T

I am a High Priestess of the Wiccan religion. I have practiced this religion for 40-plus years, but due to misconceptions by the general public, I kept my beliefs in the "broom closet", as we say, for many years. At this point in my life, I am unwilling to keep my beliefs hidden any longer. In fact, I would like to communicate to you just what it means to be Wiccan—and what it does not mean. Let's get the 'does nots 'out of the way first.

Primarily, being a witch does **not** mean that I am a devil worshiper. In fact, the Wiccan religion does not accept the existence of the devil. Satan is part of the Christian religion; he's their boy, not ours, created by that religion and its holy book. Since Wiccans are pagan, not Christian, we have absolutely nothing to do with Satan or devil worship. In contrast, Satanists are people whose religion is a perverted form of Christianity, centering on the worship of Satan, that Christian devil.

Nor do we sacrifice babies or animals. Nothing could be further from the truth. Wicca is a nature-based religion whose main focus is reverence for the earth and all its' creatures. I have never met a witch who didn't own at least one pet that was pampered and spoiled and treated like one of the family. Many are vegetarians or vegans, horrified at the practice of killing animals for food. Though I would like to be vegan, I have so many food allergies that it wouldn't work for my body.

So if we are not doing these things, what are we all about? Wicca is a broad-based religion that includes practices of various ancient pagan beliefs and ceremonies—dating back to pre-history. There are as many different paths in Wicca as there are different religious and cultural origins.

Most early religions were based on the worship of a main Goddess and a pantheon of lesser Gods and Goddesses. These religions were practiced to insure the survival of the people. Their rites focused on insuring fertility of the crops and animals, healing the sick, providing safe passage for the souls of the dead, successful hunting, winning wars against enemies, marking rites of passage, and thanking and praising their Gods and Goddesses for success in all their endeavors.

Some Definitions:

Polytheism – is the belief that there are many Gods and Goddesses. These are individual entities, in no way part of or connected to other pantheons, God or Goddess, or anything else outside of their own domain. This is the traditional way of belief for most Pagan Paths.

Unitheism – The belief that all that exists, from the most powerful Deity to the very earth we stand on is a manifestation of one Great Spirit or Universal Force. Unitheists tend to mix deities from various pagan belief systems, as they believe that all Gods are one God and tend to work with the manifestations that they are most comfortable with. Also, they tend to look for the wisdom underlying the various traditions instead of picking one tradition and following it to the exclusion of all other paths.

Elementals – Most pagans also work with the four Elements, Earth, Air, Fire and Water. Many also recognize a fifth element, Spirit. Others recognize all kinds of spirits in life around them. I can testify that animals have spirits (of course!) and so to plants. I've see tree spirits, and many people have a special feeling for trees, though they may not know why. When I was a child, I had a special tree that I would climb into and tell all my troubles to. I called it Grandfather, and it was very helpful in surviving a childhood that was not ideal.

Traditions - Many Wiccans follow a particular tradition based on their genetic heritage or their primary interests. They may choose to be Strega (Italian-based), Pictish or Caledonic (Scottish-based), Celtic (British/Irish Celtic/Druidic tradition), Gardinerian (England-based, modernized), Alexandrian (modified Gardinerian), Dianic or Elusian (Greek-based), Ceremonial (Egyptian or Quabalistic traditions), Pow-wow (Germanic-based), Seax-Wiccan (Saxon origins), Teutonic (Norse-based), Enocian (Angle-based), Shamanic (Native American or indigenous Indian based), Elemental (earth element based), Kitchen Witch (herbal healers) to name a few—and Eclectic (honoring and practicing all of the above according to the purpose of the rite or ritual, or the energy required at that time.

And why are so many beliefs and practices acceptable paths in one religion? Because as Wiccans, we primarily believe that there may or may not be only one Creator, but all is unknowable to our limited human state and simple human minds. However, all other worldly beings are accessible to us through many archetypical forms. Therefore, all forms of the Goddess and God are valid aspects of the One, and we can communicate with and offer praise to the Creator in a way we humans do understand.

Some of these archetypes were actual human beings that achieved 'Godhood' just as certain modern beings have achieved sainthood. Some are otherworldly beings. Some may even have been creations of human imagination, but since we believe in the power of thought to create, the power of collective thought and worship by thousands of people for hundreds or thousands of years have surely created these beings in some dimension or other. The "gods" of old may even have been alien visitors to our planet. The universe is large (an understatement) and almost anything could exist far beyond our planet.

Wiccans believe in the existence of other-dimensional life; the 'little people' found in the roots of so many ancient cultures, for example. Last time I checked the Hadron collider information, scientists say they have discovered (and opened) thirteen different dimensions. No word about what they found. I wonder if they really know what they are doing!

My Journey:

You might be wondering who I am, and why I am now Wiccan. As of this writing, I am a retired teacher (of many things, including dance, metaphysics, astrology, and public school) and have ALWAYS been a witch, though I didn't know what I was until I was in my late 20's.

In the early 70's I decided to offer and host a spiritual study group. Four women answered my advertisement, and we were studying meditation, extra-sensory perception and religious philosophy. I soon met an astrologer who was truly knowledgeable and competent. I was curious and interested, but the whole thing looked extremely complicated, and she was not interested in teaching me. However, she did refer me to her sister, who was willing to teach me the basics.

I found it to be a fascinating study, but there were no books on the subject in Montana at that time. I decided to remedy this by opening a metaphysical bookstore in 1973. Soon after, one of the publishing companies held an astrology conference in Minneapolis, Minnesota, which several of us decided to attend. The speakers were legendary; Robert Hand, Marcia Moore, Dan Rudhyar and several others. I was also able to order some good books for my store.

Near the end of the conference, another group was arriving to attend a conference on Wicca. I was fascinated, as I had never heard anything about this religious philosophy and was curious. I should have extended my stay and attended. Instead, few years went by before I actually looked into this religious philosophy. The following, however, is one of the things that came out of this gathering: As adopted by:

The Council of American Witches in 1974

"The council of American Witches finds it necessary to define modern Witchcraft in terms of the American experience and needs. We are not bound by traditions from other times and other cultures, and owe no allegiance to any person or power greater than the Divinity manifested through our own being. As American Witches, we welcome and respect all life-affirming teachings and traditions and seek to learn from all and to share our learning within our Council.

It is in this spirit of welcome and cooperation that we adopt these few principles of Wiccan belief. In seeking to be inclusive, we do not wish to open ourselves to the destruction of our group by those on self-serving power trips, or to philosophies and practices contradictory to those principles. In seeking to exclude those whose ways are contradictory to ours, we do not want to deny participation with us to any who are sincerely interested in our knowledge and beliefs, regardless of race, color, sex, age, national or cultural origins, or sexual preference. We therefore ask only that those who seek to identify with us accept these few basic principles.

- We practice rites to attune ourselves with the natural rhythm of the life forces marked by the phases of the moon and the seasonal quarters and cross-quarters.
- We recognize that our intelligence gives us a unique responsibility toward our environment. We seek to live in harmony with Nature, in ecological balance offering fulfillment to life and consciousness within an evolutionary concept.
- We acknowledge a depth of power far greater than is apparent to the average person. Because it is far greater than ordinary, it is sometimes called "supernatural," but we see it as lying within that which is naturally potential to all.
- We conceive of the Creative Power in the Universe as manifesting through polarity—as masculine and feminine—and that this same creative Power lives in all people and functions through the interaction of the masculine and feminine. We value neither

above the other, knowing each to be supportive of the other. We value sexuality as pleasure, as the symbol and embodiment of life, and as one of the sources of energies used in magickal practice and religious worship.

- We recognize both outer worlds and inner, or psychological worlds, sometimes known as the Spiritual World, the Collective Unconscious, the Inner planes, and we see in the interaction of these two dimensions the basis for paranormal phenomena and magickal exercises. We neglect neither one dimension nor the other, seeing both as necessary for our fulfillment.

- We do not recognize any authoritarian hierarchy, but do honor those who teach, respect those who share their greater knowledge and wisdom, and acknowledge those who have courageously given of themselves in leadership.

- We see religion, magick and wisdom-in-living as being united in the way one views the world and lives within it—a world view and philosophy of life, which we identify as Witchcraft, or the Wiccan Way.

- Calling oneself 'Witch' does not make a Witch, but neither does heredity itself, or the collecting of titles, degrees and initiations. A Witch seeks to control the forces within him/herself that make life possible in order to live wisely and well, without harm to others, and in harmony with Nature.

- We acknowledge that it is the affirmation and fulfillment of life, in a continuation of evolution and development of consciousness that gives meaning to the universe we know, and to our personal role within it.

- Our only animosity toward Christianity or toward any other religion or philosophy-of-life is to the extent that its institutions have claimed to be 'the one true right and only way' and have sought to deny freedom to others and to suppress other ways of religions practices and belief.

- As American Witches, we are not threatened by debates on the history of the Craft, the origins of various terms or the legitimacy of various aspects of different traditions. We are concerned with our present and our future.

- We do not accept the concept of 'absolute evil', nor do we worship any entity known as 'Satan' or 'the Devil' as defined by Christian Tradition. We do not seek power through the suffering of others, nor do we accept the concept that personal benefits can only be derived by denial to another.

- We work within Nature for that which contributes to our health and well-being."

Main Beliefs

Wiccan Traditions: Of course, there are many traditions with various differences:

Alexandrian – Founded in England during the 1960's by Alex Sanders. The rituals are said to be modified Gardnerian Tradition – Gerald Gardner publicized this tradition through the media in the 1950's. It is more closeted, more formal, and more structured than some others. Coven members attain degrees by study and practice with the group.

British Traditional Wicca – A mix of Celtic and Gardnerian beliefs, stemming mostly from the Farrar studies (authors of the Witch's Bible Complete from England). They are fairly structured, and heterogeneous. Members undergo a degree training process.

Caledonii Tradition – Formally known as the Hecatine Tradition, this path of the craft is of Scottish origin and preserves the unique festivals of the Scots.

Celtic Wicca – Uses a Celtic/Druidic pantheon mixed with a little ritual Gardnerian. Heavy stress is placed on the elements, nature and the Ancient Ones, use of plants, stones, flowers, trees, the mental spirits, the little people, gnomes and fairies for magickal healing and purpose.

Ceremonial Wicca –Uses a great deal of ceremonial magick in their rites and practices. This may involve Egyptian magick, or Quaballistic magick.

Dianic Wicca – Prime focus is on the Goddess and membership is for women only, but some modern circles now do allow men.

Eclectic Wicca – Eclectic witches do not follow any particular tradition, denomination, sect, or magickal practice. They learn and study from many magickal systems and apply to themselves what appears to work best.

Enocian Tradition – This uses formalized Ceremonial Magick that invokes the Angels and other-world beings for magickal purposes.

Hereditary Wicca – Those who can trace the Craft through their family tree and who have been taught the Old Religion by a living relative. Hereditary witches might adopt other individuals into their dynasty.

Kitchen Wicca – The more practical side of the tradition, using household tools and items and working with the Earth and the Elements. The hearth was the hub of creating charms and spells, healing and all celebrations.

Pow-Wow - Indigenous to South Central Pennsylvania, this system of faith healing had its roots in German Witchcraft. It is in danger of dying out.

Satanic Wicca – There is no such thing! One cannot be a satanic Witch because Witches do not believe in Satan. Satan is part of the Christian pantheon.

Seax-Wicca – In 1973, Raymond Buckland founded and authored this tradition without breaking his original Gardnerian oath. He has authored many textbooks on different magickal aspects and practices of the Craft.

Solitary Wicca – One who practices alone, regardless of tradition, denomination or sect.

Strega Wicca – Follows a tradition seated in Italy that was made public in 1353 by a witch by the name of Aradia.

Teutonic Wicca – The Teutons have been recognized as a group of people who speak the Germanic group of languages. This included the English, Dutch, Icelandic, Danish, Norwegian and Swedish peoples. This tradition is also known as the Nordic tradition and is a follower of the Odinist sect.

And, of course, there are many other magickal traditions that differ from Wicca. Here are a few…

Alchemy – This combination of chemistry, philosophy and magick is still with us today. The alchemical goal is to use a series of principles and processes which could ultimately purify the soul and distill the divine essence from crass humanity. It is a system of personal transformation.

Bruheria – A blend of Roman Catholicism, centered on the worship of Our Lady of Guadalupe (an aspect of the Virgin Mary who appeared to an Indian convert in 1531) and the Aztec Goddess faith, with sprinklings of several other magickal systems mixed in.

Hermetic Order of the Golden Dawn – Originated in 1884 with the finding of a mysterious manuscript. There is a complex hierarchy through which initiates worked to perform High Magick.

Huna – The ancient psycho-spiritual religious system of Hawaii, which had its roots in the ancestral cultures of the Berbers in North Africa.

Quabala – A magickal system of Jewish theosophy and mysticism which flourished during the middle ages, though evidence suggests its roots go much farther back.

Santeria – An offshoot of VooDoo now practiced in the United States.

Shamanism – Found in Native American nations of both continents, in Northern Europe and Asia. Practitioners are able to enter an altered state of consciousness at will in order to access the 'hidden reality' to acquire knowledge, power, and to heal or assist other.

Voudun – Also called Vodun or Voodoo refers to a religious and magickal tradition which began in Africa and later blended with Catholicism as it migrated to the West Indies and the Unites States.

Then, there is the **Wiccan Witch!**

One who believes that all of the aspects of nature are spiritual and to be honored, that there is a universal consciousness and the divine exists within all creation.

A Wiccan will adhere completely to the Wiccan Rede, along with the self-governing aspect of the Three-fold Law of Return. This means that Wiccans believe that whatever they do will be returned to them three fold, whether it be bad or good.

Wiccans believe in the return of the soul through reincarnation and in the laws of Karma.

Wiccans work with nature and the elements in order to further their knowledge and goals. They are able to enlist the help of the Elementals (other spiritual beings that exist in the natural world) out of a mutual respect for their associated powers.

Witches are not all women. The term and meaning applies to males as well.

There are many others: Candomble, Xango and Macumba of Brazil, Chinese/Taoist magick, Gypsies, the feats of the Yogis, Hindis and the Aborigines.

Much has been lost, but all these traditions and systems of belief and magickal practices follow similar ground rules and practices.

CHAPTER 4

THE THREE CORE TENANTS OF WICCA

1. Wiccans believe in reincarnation. (That works for me, because I remember several of my previous lives). We believe that the 'soul' or 'life force' continues to exist after death in a place we call Summerland (comparable to the Christian heaven). We do not believe in Hell, except of one's own making, for if a person thinks they deserve to go to Hell, they probably will —until they realize they don't really have to be there and move on.

We believe that the soul can enter a new human (or perhaps even an animal) body to gain another physical life experience. We live over and over, as many lifetimes as it takes to accomplish, or learn, or do whatever else is needed in order to advance our soul's purpose.

Wiccans have a 'live and let live' philosophy of non-exclusion. Since the one law is very clear, many things that some Christian religions call sins are just not in our book. No one is excluded, regardless of race, creed, gender or sexual orientation as long as they do their best to live by the Rede

2. Wiccans believe in magickal energy – We believe that there is a "higher power," but we do not accept that there is only one God, one Son, and one unremarkable woman that constitute deity. We believe that there may be many, and we appeal to them as forms of humans, but don't really know who or what they are – only that they seem to care about humans and try to help us through our earthly lives.

But we humans are not powerless. We are able to heal ourselves and others, to divine the future, to raise energy (positive or negative) for a variety of reasons, and create sacred space, within which we cast a circles of protection, honor the four directions and seek assistance from angels and a whole pantheon of Gods and Goddesses. I have done these things long before I ever heard of Wicca. Obviously I have been a witch in other lifetimes, and obviously, I remembered what to do and how to do it. It was quite obvious to me that this life, this body, was not the only one I've experienced.

Finally, after searching many different denominations and religions, I found my rightful place! I had been at some other time, and still was, a Witch! Not the scary kind that causes harm. The kind that sees, and senses, that humans are far more powerful than we are taught to believe.

3. We believe in the 3-fold Law of Return: Whatever you do or say will come back to you 3-fold. (I've never know if that means 3 different times, or 3 times as strong, but I don't really want to find out.) Magick (the correct spelling) is REAL, just as is prayer, so do/think/act with mindfulness that it WILL come back to you even if in another lifetime. Karma can be a bitch!

Thirteen Goals of a Witch – Author unknown

1. Know yourself
2. Know your craft
3. Learn
4. Apply knowledge with wisdom
5. Achieve balance

6. Keep your words in good order
7. Keep your thoughts in good order
8. Celebrate life
9. Attune with the cycles of the Earth
10. Breathe and eat correctly
11. Exercise the body
12. Meditate
13. Honor the Goddess and God

The Rede

*Bide the Wiccan laws ye must, In
perfect love and perfect trust.
Ye must live and let live, fairly take and fairly give.
Cast the circle thrice about, to keep unwanted spirits out.
To bind the spell well every time, let
the spell be spoken in rhyme.
Soft of eye and light of touch, speak
ye little and listen much.
Deosil go by waxing moon, chanting
out the Wiccan runes.
Widdershins go by waning moon,
chanting out the baneful tune.
When the Lady's moon is new, kiss
the hand to Her times two.*

The *"Wiccan Rede,"* which you can find all over the internet and in shops, outlines the expected behavior of a *"Witch"* It states that whatever you do will come back to you times three! This discourages using magickal practices that could cause harm.

CHAPTER 5

WHERE'S THE MAGICK?

You might hear that we cast spells. This is true, but never to control or harm, for that would violate the law we live by; the Wiccan Rede, our vow to harm none. Our spells are akin to prayers. Some are rituals of thanks, gratitude, or praise. Many are requests for meeting our own spiritual, mental, emotional or physical needs. If a person of another religion goes to church and lights a candle for a specific purpose or person, he/she is casting a spell in the same way Wiccans do. There is no difference.

Thousands of years ago, women were the important leaders and heads of the native tribes. It wasn't until the wars between tribes started that men usurped the "head of the household" positions and the status of women was lowered. In fact, these practices originated with the pagan's pre-Christian ways. The people were not willing to give up some parts of their Goddess-based religions, so some were carried over and absorbed into the new Christian (and Catholic) religions. The Goddess of old became "Mother Mary" and many of the practices, such as the burning of candles as prayer and purifying with incense, were absorbed into the "new" religion.

Magic, a core belief:

There is an impartial flow of energy from the Cosmos that is recognized in many countries by different names. This energy is available to all life; it can be utilized for good or for evil, but as witches, we understand that wrongly used, it would be returned to us threefold, and that wouldn't be pretty!

The most noticeable energies come from the Sun and the Moon, as they affect our planet most directly. I do suggest that you go to the website "electric universe.info" for more information. I think this alternative theory is absolutely accurate. They affirm that it is not gravity that rules the stars and planets; it is electrical energy. I've been to several of their conferences, listened to the scientists that support this theory, and think they are totally right! These energies are recognized in every culture, just have different names:

Chi – *Chinese term for life force or energy*

Huna - *the Hawaiian term for healing, enlightenment and personal empowerment*

Mana - *in Polynesian, the Melanesian, and Maori belief, the pervasive supernatural or magical power is known as Mana*

Personal Energy; our own energy: All living beings are energetically charged, including humans. Different cultures have different names for this energy

Prana - *life force or energy in India or Japan*

Yogi – *physical, mental and spiritual practices that originated in ancient India.*

Many forms of healing, such as Acupuncture and massage, are used today that recognize the energy of the seven chakras, or Chi points, the energy centers in the body, and the meridians, or pathways of energy that flow throughout the body. These practices are not new – they have existed for many centuries.

Kirlian aura photography, which uses special cameras and film, actually records these energy pathways and illuminates the life force in all things; people, plants, and animals.

One's own energy can be increased by the practices of meditation, physical/mental exercise, healthy eating and healthy living. This energy can be used to physically charge objects or heal others.

Environmental energy is the energy of the natural world. Our planet has its own energy system, also recognized by humanity for hundreds or thousands of years. Some names given to the energy of our planet are; Feng Shui, Dragon Lines, Ley Lines, or Aboriginal Songlines.

Places have individual energies that can be sensed as well. You feel this when you enter a holy place, or visit a battlefield or other place where terrible things have happened. I was in Italy once, and visited a large, beautiful church. But I was horrified, because I could sense the dungeons below and the torture that "witches" endured during the burning times. I couldn't get out of there fast enough! Some places are holy and glorious to experience, but others are definitely haunted as well.

Every part of nature, plants, rocks, trees, bodies of water – all of nature vibrates with energy. When we eat raw foods, we ingest this energy, which is healthy for our bodies and souls. Some is lost when food is cooked, but not everything is good, or good for you (meat) in the raw state.

Universal energy; But that isn't all. Deities exist in all dimensions. Some have wonderful, uplifting, spiritual energy. Gods and Goddesses, angels and demons, all exist and have either a positive or negative energy. As witches, we honor these ethereal beings, and work with the positive ones in ritual. In fact, you should never use only your own energy in ritual. Work with the positive forces that are in alignment with the purpose of your own ritual. They will help you create the "Cone of Power" needed to work effective magick.

It would be really, really stupid to work with the negative ones, because whatever you do, remember, will return to you threefold!!!

Deity – Spiritual Energy

All the ancient religions, with the possible exception of the Norse, worshiped the Goddess. The God was her consort, but he represented the cycle of life, death, and rebirth. The Goddess changed form; from Maiden to Mother to Crone, but was an omnipotent being; always present and always powerful! As mentioned, this changed when warriors became the most essential members of the tribe. During this time, the feminine deities sort of took a back seat to the males.

Connecting with any of these god forms ads a special, almost ecstatic, energy that can help make a ritual or spell most effective and uplifting. This is a practice that was part of all the "old" religions throughout history. Some evangelistic sects today still raise this energy and hopefully put it to good use.

CHAPTER 6

THE WHEEL; EVER CHANGING, NEVER ENDING!

One important difference in our religion is the 'Wheel of the Year'. Our rituals, ceremonies and lives are always timed to the changing of the seasons, the ever-rotating wheel of time that governs this planet. Plant-sow-reap; these things were all-important to our ancestors who could not pop down to the corner store if they needed something—whose very existence depended on the whims of nature, the success of the crops and flocks. We 'civilized' people have lost that all-important connection to Mother Earth. In that process, we have lost respect for her as well, and continue to rape and pollute her without caring or realizing that if she dies, so will we. Many Wiccans are active environmentalists, fighting to save her wherever they can.

Many of the ancient ceremonies and practices that marked the turning of the seasons have been incorporated into Christian holidays and celebrations. Ask any Jehovah's Witness—their research is correct (on this, at least). The Pagan holidays live on in disguise. But those of us who wish to return to the roots of religion have chosen to tear away that disguise and return to the true purposes of these celebrations. And celebrate we do, with beautiful rituals, costumes, dance, song, music, fire circles, love and joy! And all without the use of illegal drugs or excessive consumption of alcohol!

Behold, the Wheel!

Ever changing, never ending
8 portals of the year attending!
Marking days and passing time
To honor the Lord and Lady sublime.

Begins the year at Hallow's Eve
Departed ones we meet and grieve
Looking deep within our hearts
As the Sun King thus departs.
We search our souls through darkest night
And seek the answers to our plight.
Gone 'till Yule, when He returns
As light within, to flicker and burn

He strengthens and grows with Imbolg's approach
This Goddess welcomes, with no reproach.
And hope begins to lighten the land
As fertile flocks and fields are planned.
And Oestara brings the promise of life,
And dreams abound to overcome strife.
We bless the creatures and the Earth
As the cycle continues of life and birth.

As Beltane fires burn, we salute the Spring,
The divine couple and all that they bring.
We honor the fairies and Otherworld creatures,
And welcome the Green Man with foliate features.

The Sun King is strong and energy high
The daylight long when Litha comes nigh.
Tend to your crops—whatever they be
And harvest the first of your fields merrily.

The burning of Lugh and the first harvest bread
Mark Lughnasadh with joy—and the Sun King with dread
As he grows weaker, the light to wane,
He gravely forsees the end of his reign.

At Mabon we give thanks for all that has been
Knowing the wheel must turn yet again.
Now light and dark even, the ageing King fades,
The fields soon lie fallow, the darkness pervades.
Constant through all, the Goddess is nigh,

Her symbol, the moon, marks the months in the sky.
Her influence guides us throughout the year,
Her love and her magick always are near.
Thus complete, the cycle of time
Spoken as Magick, spoken in rhyme.

By Charlyn Scheffelman

CHAPTER 7

THE SABBATS: OUR
MAJOR HOLIDAYS

As Pagans, we celebrate the traditional holidays, but in any form that appeals to us. We are eclectic, so we can celebrate any and all traditions of the past (or present) that we choose. Beautiful rituals that honor deity from any part of the world and any time period still honors our ancestors and the god forms we wish to acknowledge. No one really knows what the divine is, but we know that we can feel the divine energy, no matter what we call it as long as we are sincere in our rituals and worship, and celebrations.

Samhain

Our year begins with Halloween or Samhain (pronounced 'sou-when', or 'so-ween'). The name is probably derived from the Aryan God of Death, **S**amana, or the Irish/Gaelic "samhraidhreadh" which translates to "summer's end." Many of the things we do, honor, or celebrate come from other ancient traditions.

This period is the beginning of the dark season, when darkness is longer than light each day. In some cultures this represents the death of the Sun God. He is also seen as Old Father Time. This is the time of the "Dark Mother," the most powerful aspect of the ancient Goddess, the Crone.

Unlike the Sun God, the Goddess never dies. The Crone morns the death of the Sun God for the following six weeks; known as the Reign of Darkness (winter) because the Sun God is in the "underworld." His rebirth will be at Yule, around December 22nd, (Christmas). This is in line with the belief in reincarnation, and the cycle of light and darkness, life and death.

The Goddess never dies, but she changes form during the year; from the Dark Mother (the Crone or Old Wise Woman), to the Mother who gives birth to the Sun on December 21, when the Sun's journey South becomes noticeable and days grow longer. The Goddess then becomes the Maiden in Spring, ready to love again, as the Earth's orbit brings us nearer the sun, and the cycle repeats.

Samhain was one of the High Festivals for the Celts, along with Imbolg, Beltane, and Laughnassadh; all were "fire festivals". All fires were extinguished, then were relit from a central "Druid fire". The turning point from light into darkness signified the New Year. It was also a time when the departed souls could return and visit, and a time for divination.

Halloween night was considered to be a night of chaos, neither part of the old year nor part of the new year. The tricksters (resentful Fairy Folk) would play their tricks on humans, create mischief, and even kidnap humans and take them to the land of the fey. It was a time when departed ones could visit (and were given a feast of welcome), as the gates to the land of the dead (Tir nan Og) were open. It was also a time for various forms of divination.

In Mexico, El Dia de Muerte (The Day of the Dead) was celebrated two days after Samhain. This was traditionally an Aztec festival, honoring Mictecacihuatl, the "Lady of the Dead" and Huitzilopochtli, an Aztec war deity. It was also a time to honor the ancestors, and to eat and drink, and specifically consume chocolate to wish the dead a "sweet return" in their next incarnation.

They toast a personification of "Death" on his day off! They honor departed ones by having picnics at their graves, decorating the graves, burning candles and torches, and telling stories about their ancestors. It's a celebration that ranges somewhere between a holiday to ancestor worship!

Rome celebrates with a sort of "up-side-down day". Slaves act as kings, and kings act as slaves. They celebrate the Apple Goddess, Pomona, and Fortuna, the Goddess of Wealth and Luck. They also see this as a time to visit the "Land of the Dead," and the time when departed spirits can crossover and return for our celebrations. Of course, there were rituals, feasts, and lots (and lots) of drinking alcohol!

In Norse lands, the trickster Loki, the "father of lies" was honored. He was said to be an attractive, cunning, witty, dangerous, unpredictable, deceitful shape changer.

Anansi the Spider was honored in Africa, and Hermes led the dead to the underworld. He was their God of luck, magick and fortune, and was the patron of alchemists.

Other deities present and honored at this time are:

Mercury, the thieving, magickal, cunning mischief maker and messenger of Roman origin.

Siksa, a Slavic forest sprite

Kapua, a Hawaiian shape shifter with great strength and multiple magickal powers, but also a trickster and mischief maker.

Maui of the thousand tricks, a shape shifter and magician in Polynesia.

Susanoo, mischief maker, God of storms, thunder, and earthquakes in Japan.

Old, old Coyote, God of Gaiety, physical sex, and irrational fun. He was an uncontrolled trickster God of the Aztecs.

North American Native Americans, **Coyote** and **Raven** were tricksters sometimes call the trickster, demon-clown

European tricksters include the **Lord of Misrule**, a spirit of fun that caused pleasant havoc, as did the **Abbot Unreason, the King of Bean, Jester,** and **the Master of Merry Disport.**

These old deities are the reason we have "Tricks or Treats" as a major part of this holiday!

Of course, with the arrival of Christianity, other ways to celebrate in a more accepted style resulted in Michaelmas, the feast day of St. Michael. The 7th Century C.E. change moved All Saints Day to November first as well. The Eve of All Saints, or All Hallows Eve, promoted honoring the Christian God and all his Saints.

Hallowmass was a religious mass to honor the dead, and All Souls Day on November 2, was designated as time to offer prayers for departed ones. The church promoted the rumors that pagans were "evil" people who caused everything from disease to accidents using black magick, and the Wise Woman, or Crone, was then portrayed as an evil, ugly old woman.

In Wicca, the land of the dead is called Summerland. Halloween eve is the time that the veils between worlds are thinnest, and contact with departed ones is easier, as they are also at Beltane, Samhain's opposite holiday. Dumb Suppers are held. This is a silent meal. Each participant invites an ancestor or other departed person to the celebration. The High Priestess meditates for 13 days on reaching each spirit guest previous to the event, inviting them to attend.

Beside each person is an empty seat and plate meant for their otherworldly guest. The guest's and the attendee's plates are filled with foods which are said to appeal to spirits. The HPS calls the guests, inviting them into the circle, and the meal is consumed in silence. When the HPS feels that the communication is complete, she sends the guests back to the netherworld with gratitude, and opens the circle she had cast for the event.

Samhain is: *a time for Divination

*a time to wrap up old projects, and take stock of one's self and life

*a time to initiate winter projects, do research, or handicrafts

It is also the time of the wise old Crone and her Cauldron of rebirth, and a time for meditation, self-searching and preparing and planning for the coming year.

Yule

Yule is a Pagan holiday that, according to anthropologist E. W. Budge, is 12,000 years old. It celebrates the rebirth of the Sun God (or Goddess). Others say it goes back even further and celebrates the "return" of the Sun from its furthest distance from our planet. This is the beginning of warmer days for (part of) Earth.

This holiday was celebrated in Rome, Greece, Persia, Egypt and Asia Minor as the "birthday of the invincible Sun," Mithras. He was said to be "born in a barn to a virgin (which in those days meant an independent woman). He was the "Child of the God of all Gods" and his followers prayed for his return, as he was seen to be the bringer of new life.

In Rome, as Romans were inclined to do, Saturnalia was a twelve-day festival! It also was celebrated as the New Year. Gifts were given and people "bathed in gold" as a spell for prosperity. This also translated to the giving of gold coins at Hanukah, and the "Feast of Light".

In lands of the Norse, this was a 12-night celebration as well. The Goddess Sunna (also known as Sol, Sul, Sulis, Sulla, and Sel) was the goddess who guides the Sun. The "First Night" or "Mother Night" was celebrated as the birth of the Sun Goddess, Freya. It was also seen as the beginning of the new year. They believed that Holde, the guardian of the Spirit world, opened the door between the worlds so that spirit contact with ancestors was possible.

Father Thor gives gifts and answered prayers. He wears red, has magickal tools and rides the skies in a chariot pulled by magickal steeds. He lives in "Asgard with his wife, Sif, who nurtures us with baked goodies, breads, cookies and cakes. "Toasts and boasts" are given with mead or cider, and fire is honored, often by rolling a burning wheel, "the Sun wheel" downhill.

*In Egyptian lore, Nun, the primordial black sea of chaos (the womb) birthed Ra, the Sun God. He in turn, birthed other deities and cried dark tears that became humans. The beginning of the "rainy season" is said to be Ra's tears.

*Some Native American tribes celebrated "Soyalanwul" a term which meant "to bring new life to the world." They performed the birthing ritual of the Sun God, which symbolized the" birth" by the physical act of a masked person crawling between the legs of the tribe's women.

*Germany celebrated Frau Holde, who rode the wind on a sleigh, giving out gifts of gold. She particularly rewarded the spinners of fine cloth. And no rotary action of any kind was permitted on Yule Eve until St. Catherine's wheel was set on fire and rolled downhill.

*Anglo-Saxons celebrated "Yula" or Yule. On this night, the Goddess becomes the Virgin Mother. This celebration was held on the longest night of the year and honors the return of the sun and longer days. Candles are lit as "sympathetic" magick (using an element to influence that element). They also burned the "Yule log."

*The Celts sacrificed a strong oak tree and burned the fire all night, coaxing the sun to return. "Wren boys" solicited money to bury "Wren" by Robin in their cultural tail.

Wiccan Holidays are also tied to the seasons. As Wiccans, we celebrate the "Wheel of the Year," which represents the circle of time on our planet. A wreath (wheel) is decorated with Evergreen (for lasting life), holly (for fertility), mistletoe (cut by Druids with a golden sickle on the 6th night of the moon), and bay leaves (good fortune) which was sacred to Sol (the Sun God of Rome) and Apollo (the Greek God who drove the Sun chariot) and bells, which was a Norse tradition, used to scare away the powers of darkness.

Carols are sung and we make our plans for the New Year.

The First Yule—Author Unknown

Once upon a time, long, long ago, a beautiful young woman lived on a blue and green island. She had many friends on the island, fairies, trees, flowers, rabbits, deer and birds… but she was the only person who lived there. She wanted to share her friends and her secrets with other people just like her, so she began to give birth. Every month when the moon was hiding, she gave birth. For the first six months, she gave birth to daughters with dark skin and eyes. For the last six moons of the year she gave birth to fair skinned daughters. On the seventh moon of every year the First Mother gave birth to a magickal, sacred oak.

As the years turned, many, many daughters were born, and quite a few oak trees as well. The daughters played games with the animals and each other; they climbed in the branches of the oak trees and gathered flowers with the fairies. One day, the first born daughter of the First Mother gave birth herself. The First Mother was very proud and happy. Her favorite friend, Oak Tree (who was very wise), gave her a silver crown to wear and told her that she was now a Grandmother. Soon many of the daughters gave birth, and the island became an even happier place, full of babies and big girls and mommies who all played together with the animals, the trees and the fairies.

One winter night when the moon was hiding, one of the daughters gave birth to a baby that was different from anything they had ever known. It was not a daughter, it was not even an oak tree; it was a baby BOY! It was a very dark cold night, the longest winter's night of the year, so all the daughters and all the animals were snuggled up together to keep cozy and warm. After their excitement of seeing a brand new baby born passed, the daughters and the animals realized that the baby boy was not feeling well. He was not as strong or as warm as the babies and trees that were usually born on the island. They all began to worry about the new baby, and tried to help keep him warm. The animals with the furriest coats pushed up close to the mother and baby, the fairies sprinkled magick dust above him, and the little girls sang wonderful songs and danced around and around the room...

Another interesting piece is: "_A Gift to the Magi, Explained_" by Jeffery L. Sheler, published in the U.S. News & World Report, Dec. 20. 1999.

Imbolc

The most popular identity for this holiday currently is Groundhog Day, but for the church it became Candlemass, and for the general public, Valentine's Day. The date ranges from January 31 to February 2.

In Wicca, Imbolg (an optional spelling) is one of the eight "Greater Sabbats". But let's just go with Pagan Valentine's Day. (It was originally "Galentine's Day", honoring gallant, dashing young men and their many love affairs.) In the middle ages, the letter "g" was a "v", thus galantine became valentine. If you haven't guessed by now, this is the first fertility festival of the year, as six weeks after giving birth in December, the maiden is ready to love again.

Brigit (Bridget, Briged, Bride or The Exalter One) was the daughter of Dagda, the Great God, and Danu, the Mother Goddess. She was the Goddess of Fire and the Patroness of smith craft, as well as poetry, healing, birth, divination, prophecy, domestic animals and agriculture. She is a triple goddess; the maiden aspect of Danu. She was accompanied by two magickal oxen.

Oimelc was an early name for this holiday. It celebrated the lactating ewes, whose milk provided a staple food. The people celebrated spring and the first stirrings of life, as flowers blossomed and the lambing season began. Offerings of milk and honey were made to the fields, bonfires were laid and candles were blessed.

In Scotland, the crone goddess, Cailleach, was reborn as Bride. An old passage thus describes: 'Bride with her white wand is said to breathe life into the mouth of the dead Winter God, and to bring him to open his eyes to the tears and the smiles, the sighs and the laughter of Spring. The venom of the cold is said to tremble for its safety on Bride's Day and then flee for its life on St Pat Day.' (D.J. Conway).

Cailleach was reborn as Bride. The Roman equivalent goddess was Venus. This was a cleansing time, associated with the goddess of "fresh starts," Febua, whose name is associated with February.

In the Norse lands, the holiday was called the Disting-tid, a time to prepare the earth with salt, ashes, and sacred herbs for the planting ahead. The people of Greece honored the goddess Diana, who was also the Goddess of Love.

Converting this holiday to Christianity was not too hard, as the young Goddess could be associated with the Virgin Mary. Since she birthed the mid-winter sun (Son), and women were considered to be unclean until six weeks after giving birth, early February was the supposed time that she presented her baby (Christ) to the temple. He was called the "Light of the World." The celebrations of the time involve processions of light.

But it is also St. Bridget's Day on February 1. She was the daughter of a Druid, born in a threshold and bathed in the milk of a white, red-eared cow. She was the Goddess of fertility, childbirth, and healing. She is also known as Brigit of Kildare, whose ever-burning fire in the temples was tended by 19 nuns. No men were allowed to come near. Feasts and rites were wide spread, celebrating life after winter.

In Scotland, she was known as Mary's midwife. She had the ability to turn water into ale, and stone into salt. They also kept her Holy fire burning perpetually. It was said that her skull was kept at Kildare (this was a pre-Christian custom), but it had been stolen.

In Portugal, the cattle were driven past the holy fire to ensure fertility. German Settlers (1700) in America kept lit candles in their windows that had been blessed the Clergy during the dark of winter.

This holiday is halfway between Winter Solstice and the equinox, and was thought to forecast the coming winter. The English rhyme says:

"If Candlemas be fair and bright,
Winter has another Flight.
If Candlemas brings clouds and rain,
Winter will not come again."

And in Scotland:

"If Candlemas Day is bright and clear,
There'll be two winters in the year."

And in Germany:

"For as the sun shines on Candlemas Day,
So far will the snow swirl until May.
For as the snow glows on Candlemas Day,
So far will the sun shine before May."

And in America:

"If the sun shines on Groundhog Day;
Half the fuel and half the hay."

The German people watched the badger for his shadow. On February 4, 1841, storekeeper James Morris' wrote in his diary;

"Last Tuesday, the 2nd was Candlemas Day, the day on which, according the Germans, the Groundhog peeps out of his winter quarters and if he sees his shadow he pops back for another six weeks nap, but if the day be cloudy, he remains out, as the weather is to be moderate." Morgantown, Berks County PA.

This tradition concerning the groundhog became official, in 1886, with the yearly appearance of Punxsutawney Phil, "Seer of Seers, Sage of Sages, Prognosticator of Prognosticators, and Weather Prophet extraordinary"

In 1723, the Delaware Indians settled their camp in Punxsutawney, Pennsylvania, bringing with them the legend of Wojak, the groundhog. They saw groundhogs as their honorable ancestors, and called them 'grandfather.' They later substituted the groundhog for the badger.

In Ancient Greece and Rome, February 15th was the celebration of the God Pan, or the Festival of Lupercalia. Pan was a horned god, the oldest god in Greece; the God of the Woodland. He was seen as the positive life force of the world. He was the ruler of nature spirits, male sexuality, animals, fertility, music, dance, farming, and agriculture. He also had a "dark side," that made people fear him.

His festival was a fertility festival. Naked rites were held, Priests whacked young women with sticks, and goats were sacrificed.

The Wiccan Sabbat of Imbolc occurs on February 2nd. Candles are made and consecrated and are lit in windows to call back the light. They can also be worn as a crown, an old Scandinavian custom.

This is a time of cleansing, both spiritually and physically. Rededications are made and spiritual cleansings practiced to purify one's home and one's self. It is also time to reassess one's "stores" and replenish necessary items, review one's life and practices, reflect on one's life and path, etc.

Crafting things made for oneself or ones house, including weaving wheat crosses for protection or making corn dollies insured renewal and prosperity in the coming months.

It is also a time to make offerings to the Earth and give thanks for her gifts. Bless your plants and seeds, and plant seedlings indoors if you have a garden to move them to in the spring. Bless the food in your pantry, and maybe most importantly, meditate on what you would like to see grow in your life!

Oestara

Oestara is the Spring Equinox, around March 21, opposite Mabon, and day and night are again equal in length. It is considered to be the first day of spring; the theme is one victory and resurrection, as new life burgeons forth with the coming of warmer weather. Symbolically, the battle has now been won by the Oak King. It is the second fertility festival, and the Maiden presides. Earth's energies quicken in the spring, and new life appears in the plant and animal kingdoms. This was also the time when farms were bought and sold.

The Easter holiday is named after Eostre, a Saxon Goddess of fertility. This holiday was not an important one in Celtic lands until the Norse invasion, whereas in Greece, Rome, Nordic and German lands, it was already of great importance. Eostre/Oestara was of equal status to the God, her lover, and was impregnated by him, bringing new life to the land and animals. The Celts renamed this holiday "Lady Day" honoring the official return of the Goddess from her hibernation.

Also at this time, England honored the Lord of the Greenwood and the Green Goddess. Oestara, the German Goddess of fertility, was honored with feasts and ritual sex. The virgin Goddess of the Norse mates with young the God. The Phrygian mother goddess of mountaintops and caverns, Cybele, was impregnated by a magic almond and bore a son, Attis. Attis dies of self castration though Zeus preserved his body.

On the vernal equinox in Rome, eunuch priests had a 4-day ritual. On the first day, pine trees were brought into the temple. Day two involved much trumpeting, and on the third day, they slash their arms in a mourning ritual, then engage in frenzied music and dancing. Day four is one of rejoicing, as the God has risen.

One well-known Goddess was Persephone, daughter of Demeter, Goddess of the harvest, well known and loved by the Greeks. According to the myth, one day Persephone did not come home after playing in the fields. Demeter learned that she had been abducted by Hades, God of the Underworld! Unable to get any help from the other Gods, Demeter went on strike! She refused to bless the crops and insure a bountiful harvest. Because of failing crops, the people begged Zeus for help. He sent Hermes, the messenger to bring her back, but the law was, if she had eaten anything she could not return.

But woe, she had eaten the seeds of a pomegranate! Zeus decided that Persephone would have to stay with Hades in the underworld for two-thirds of the year, but could rejoin her mother in the springtime. Demeter was so happy that she blessed all growing things, but when Persephone had to return to the underworld, the trees dropped their leaves, and frost and snow covered the ground. Thus, our seasons are what they are.

In Slavic lands, the theme is that death has no power over the living! This is symbolized by killing and throwing a personification of death into moving water, celebrating with flowers and songs which were seen as symbols of life renewed. They passed red eggs to each other as they processed to the site of the party! If someone died on Ostara, they were said to have special treatment in the afterlife until they reincarnated.

Egypt celebrated the Feast of Isis, and Greece named it Aphrodite Day or the Festival of Athena, and Greece, Rome and Persia celebrated the Festival of Astarte. Rome's wild party was called Hilaria!

The lamb was sacred to almost all of the virgin goddesses of Europe, the Middle East and North Africa. The Easter Bunny was the goddess Eostre's patron animal, as was the hare. Legends say these animals laid sacred eggs in the God's honor. They were gaily decorated and given as offerings to the Goddess. These eggs were considered sacred and were not to be eaten by ordinary mortals in Rome, and were symbols of the corn in Germany, Holland, France and Ireland. They were taken into the fields to double the yield.

The Scots, placed a nail and an egg in sowing basket to bring fertility. The Germans smeared their ploughs with egg. They were rumored to correct impotence and sterility, and were often used in love spells and divination. (Decorated goose eggs were found in Germany from 320 A.D.). They were symbols of fertility and new life, often so in creation myths.

Wiccans often charge and bless seeds for fruitfulness, decorate eggs and charge them to represent success; goals and wishes, wear circlets of flowers, light fires, ring bells and celebrate new life.

Christian Traditions

Christians called this holiday Easter, which was celebrated on the first Sunday after the first full moon following Equinox. The theme was the "resurrection of life," beginning with Lent, a time to mourn, followed by rejoicing. One symbol was the Easter Lily, which could symbolize death, though in Rome, it served as an engagement ring and symbol of life.

It is traditional to have new clothes, even though the "Easter Bonnet" is fading as years go by. Why? Because in the past, it was bad luck not to have new clothes, which were made in secret and brought out on Easter Sunday.

Beltane (May Day)

Our fifth Sabbat celebration of the wheel occurs on May first. It is a Celtic festival known as Bealtaine in Ireland or Bealtuinn in Scottish (Galic). This is also a fertility festival that heralds the beginning of summer. It is generally held on May eve, and was seen as the triumph of light over darkness.

In Celtic lands, it was a Druidic fire festival, honoring the God of Light or Fire, known as Bel, Beli, or Belinus (and possibly Baal). At this time, they moved the flocks to their summer pastures and drove the cattle between Beltane fires to purify and protect them.

It was the marriage celebration of the Goddess (the pregnant Mother) and the Horned God, god of the forest and wildwood. Many "Handfastings" (marriages) were held on this holiday.

The people would "jump the Beltaine fire" and make love in the greenwood. This practice kept the tribe's gene pool varied, which kept the tribe's gene pool varied. Pregnancies from these unions often went by the surnames of Jackson (Jack O' the Green), Hodson (Hod=sprites), or Robinson (Robin Hood).

Boughs of Hawthorn and spring flowers were retrieved from the woods, with which they blessed the fields and the flocks. Celebrations with food and drink followed, and the May Queen and King were selected. Parades were held, and it was also the custom to eat a blackened piece of "Beltain Cake" and leap over the Beltane fire three times.

The May Pole was a tradition in the Cult of Cybele. It was a phallic symbol decorated with long red and white streamers and flowers at the top. People would dance to the accompaniment of bells as they wound the pole with the red and white streamers. This was likely an offshoot of the "world tree," or the staff found in other cultures.

The church repurposed the maypole, dubbing it the Holy Rood, or the Cross, and the May Queen became Mary. No longer was it "Rood Day."

The Green Man is another figure associated with this holiday. Green was the color of vegetation, and the coming of new leaves in spring was celebrated as revival of the trees and plants that had been dormant and leafless all winter. Often a man covered in green branches or leaves was the symbolic figure of new vegetation, and he was either sprinkled with or dunked in water to ensure there would be enough rain to bring all vegetation to fruition, providing food for the people and the animals.

In Wales, Creiddylad was celebrated as the "May Queen," the Goddess of summer flowers and love. The Balefires burned for three days and three nights, tended by the warriors at night.

In Germany, this holiday was named Walpurgisnacht (Walpurgis Night) and was the "Night of the Witches," or "Night of the Dead." Their name for the goddess of Mother Earth was Walburga. She married and was and pregnant by the god. Catholics used this name for an Anglo-Saxon missionary. She was canonized on 1 May c. 870 by Pope Adrian II.

Pagans lit fires atop hills where they practiced their rites, inviting their deceased ancestors to attend. They would chop down a tree and decorated it with egg shells and ribbons, much as we do at Christmas.

England celebrated this day with Morris dancing and Mummers plays, and the goddess became Lady Godiva. For 300 years, a nude village maiden rode through Coventry on a white horse, but the Puritans stopped this practice and the Maypole became illegal in 1644.

Rome celebrated 'Floriala' for Flora and Bacchanalia for Bacchus. Floriala was a three-day celebration April 28-May 1. It was a celebration to honor the flowers that bring fruit.

The people would clean and purify the temples and make offerings of flowers at springs and rivers. They would dance, sing, and drink all last year's flower wine. They gathered blossoms for new wine, indulged in strip teases and lewd games. It was a celebration of Bacchanalia, God of wine and frolic. Edelweiss was given as an engagement flower.

Italian celebrations included climbing a greased pole for money and the cheese at the top. (Trees represented the land of milk and honey). In Russia, the balefires were lit at moonrise and kept burning until Sunrise. Norse traditions included the lighting of Balder's fires, as he was their Sun God. Old brooms were burned and new ones were dedicated. Everyone slept at home and kept the hearth fires burning 'til dawn.

The month of May was named for Maia, a Greek mountain nymph, mother of Hermes, the God of Magick. Pictures and references to Pan, the Horned God of Western Europe and Cernunnos of the Celts were found on Eurasian cave walls and even among the hieroglyphs in Egypt.

Wiccans celebrate the coming of spring, and wind the May Pole if they have one.

Litha (Summer Solstice)

Of course, Summer Solstice is directly opposite Yule on June 20-21, and is the longest day of the year. The Sun King is at his zenith, and the Oak King loses the battle with the Holly King.

Litha is the first harvest/fire festival in the year, and is also celebrated by some as St. John's birthday, (directly opposite that of Christ). Lugh had escaped an early death when King Balor ordered his men to drown him as a child, but they refused to do so. He grew to be a legendary "Jack of all trades," warrior and Saint. He is the only Saint whose birth is celebrated instead of his death, and is actually the 'pagan' figure known as the Oak King. He is connected with the wilderness and is often shown as horned…even sometimes as a satyr, with hooves.

In England and Western Europe, this is the first fire festival of the year. The people jump over fire, hoping to ward off evil. The church portrayed faeries as dangerous beings but another tradition says if you gather fern seed at midnight and rub it on your eyelids, you will be able to see them. People would wear garlands of flowers and carry lanterns to the fire, jump over the fire and do protections spells for the animals.

In Wales and the Celtic communities, this was Gathering Day. Herbs were important for cooking, for healing, and for magick. Mistletoe was sacred to many people, and Lavender was especially used for love magick. Vervain and pine cones were used for protection and for fertility and/or virility. The rooster was sacred to the sun god and was honored in many daytime celebrations.

It was considered unlucky to marry during the month of May, so June weddings became very popular, even yet today. Wedding cake, flowers and rice were considered fertility magick. Brides would wear white dresses in honor of the Virgin Goddesses, and the wedding ring was a symbol of the magick circle in pagan religions. The Garter was a symbol of the wreath and cycle of the year, and grooms carried away their brides as an expression of fertility and prosperity.

In the Mediterranean area, the god Pan and the Forest Goddess were important deities. Pan enticed nymphs and maidens for his pleasure.

In Greece and Rome, mock funerals for the sun were held, knowing that it now began its journey north. It also marked the start of the harvest time. The Norse would Process to the ritual site with their animals, family members and torches. They gathered ash sticks to make wands and staves. Divination and vision quests were important.

This was the year's principle festival in India, and Native American tribes danced to bless the harvest. The Navajo held a 9-day feast and night Chant Dance that lasted from dusk to dawn.

In the Wiccan tradition, the God and Goddess are seen as the mature King and Queen. Healing rituals are held and protective amulets are made. It is time to cut divining rods, dowsing rods and wands, to make protective amulets and honor the Faery folk. Rituals sometimes enact the Battle of Holly and Oak Kings, or an attempted abduction of the Queen. Handfastings are performed for couples from the year before, herbs are gathered with a bowline, milk (lactation) is substituted for wine, and Mugwort is placed under ones pillow for dreams.

The Celts did not see the fairies as cute little beings; they saw them as mischievous trouble-makers that could (and would) kidnap mortals and take them away for seven years. It is said that bells and daisy chains were both effective protection against them.

In Scotland, all fires were extinguished, and then were relit by nine men using the nine sacred woods: Birch for the Goddess, oak for the God, fir for birth, willow for death, rowan for magick, apple for love, grapevine for joy, hazel for wisdom, hawthorn for purity (and for May). Then all lit their torches and twirled them overhead, ate Beltane cake, and jumped the fire three times to celebrate the triumph of light over darkness.

Wales honored Creiddylad, the May Queen, Goddess of summer flowers and love. The Balefires, tended by warriors at night, burned for three days and nights. Germany celebrated Walpurgisnacht (Walpurgis Night, Night of the Witches, Night of the Dead). They celebrated the Mother Earth Goddess, Walburga, who was married to and impregnated by the God. Fires were lit atop hills, where they practiced their rites and invited in their ancestors. They would chop down a tree and decorate it with egg shells and ribbons. Church fathers exchanged the Pagan maypole for the Holy Rood; the Cross, and called this holiday Rood Day Mary was substituted for the Queen of the May.

In England, Morris dancing and Mummers plays were popular, and for 300 years, a nude village maiden rode through Coventry on white horse as Lady Godiva. This was banned by the Puritans, and Maypoles became illegal in 1644. However, Queen Guinevere, who went 'a-Maying, was a suitable substitute.

In Rome, Floriala was a three-day celebration (April28-May1) in honor of the Goddess, Flora. The temples were cleaned and purified and decorated with flowers that bring fruit. People made offerings of flowers at springs and rivers. There was dancing, singing, and drinking all the old flower wine. They gathered blossoms for new wine and entertainment included strip teases and lewd games. Edelweiss was given as an engagement flower.

Bacchanalia, God of wine and frolic was present as well in Italy. People would climb a greased pole for the money and cheese at the top as trees were considered to be from the land of milk and honey. Young men attempted to clime the pole and reap the rewards at the top.

In Russia, balefires were lit at moonrise. Then they would throw in holly sprigs and herbs for incense.

The Norse lit Balder, the Sun God's, fires, and burned old brooms. New ones were dedicated. They all slept at home and kept the hearth fires burning 'til dawn.

May is named for Maia, a Greek mountain nymph and mother of Hermes, the God of Magick, who can be compared to Pan, the Horned God of Western Europe or Cernunnos of the Celts. Maia can also be found on Eurasian cave walls and in some Egyptian hieroglyphs.

Lughnassadh (Lammas)

Lughnassadh is one of the eight "Greater Sabbats." It is on July third and is also known as Loaf-Mass, likely because it is the harvest of the grain, which puts bread on our tables. Here begins the decline of summer, as shorter days forewarn the coming of winter.

This holiday is named after Lugh – but who is Lugh? He was given the title Ba'al, which meant owner, or lord, but the term also came to mean deity. However, this holiday is actually dedicated to Lugh's foster mother, Tailtiu. It was not uncommon, in fact it was an honor to be fostered to someone of higher standing, and Tailtiu was the last queen of the fir bolg (colonizers from Greece or Spain). She died from the great effort it took to clear the forests for farmland. Competitions (funeral games) were held in her honor, as she had requested. These events included artisans who came to exhibit their wares.

The Druids, at that time, were the court system. They settled claims for the people, determined victim's rights and decided the restitution for wrongdoing. Punishment for wrongdoers included banishment, generally by being put out to sea without oars, or being given a dangerous assignment.

Handfastings were marriages. In fact, "bride" was the term for the mother aspect of the Goddess Brid. Adonis was an early Grain God in the Assyrian, Babylonian, and Phoenicians pantheons. He was born from a Myrrh tree and was the consort of Aphrodite, the Goddess of love (known as Astarte in Phoenicia). He also spent six months of the year in Hades with Persephone.

Wales honored Llew, the son of Arainrhod, who was Goddess of the stars and reincarnation, harvest broth, ale and beer, and Freyja, Lady of Giver of the loaf, who was a Norse Goddess.

Ireland celebrated Colcannon Sunday this time of year by digging up the potatoes, a staple food for the Irish. They would wear a white apron, cook and mash the potatoes with onion, garlic or cabbage, smother them with butter and feast! The cook was given the honor of eating right from the pot. If you were wealthy, the potatoes would be accompanied by meat and seasonal fruits.

Mabon (Mabinogion)

Mabon is the third and final harvest festive of the year. It is held on the Autumn Equinox, about September 21-22. It has been called the Wiccan Thanksgiving and was originally honoring the Welsh God, Mabon.

Mabon, the son of Modron, was kidnapped when he was only three days old. No one knew where he had been taken. However, he was enjoying a pleasant life in his Mother's womb in the Otherworld. There he was nurtured, renewed, and reborn. This parallels the seeds that fall, or that we plant this time of year to come up in the spring.

The Celtic story concerning the death of Lugh, who sacrificed himself for his people, has an astrological parallel. The astrological sign of Libra is represented by a balance scale. Some representations show a youth standing "on the balance", with one foot on a goat (Capricorn) and the other on the cauldron (Cancer). Lugh was betrayed by Blodeuwedd (the Virgin, or Virgo) and turned into an eagle (Scorpio.)

Eleventh Century Welsh tales concerning this holiday were written down and translated first in 1838-1849. They were oral tales of unknown origin, passed down from ancient times. These tales became the basis of the Arthurian legends.

This celebration became Harvest Home, and Anglo-Celtic harvest festival, during which the grain was threshed and the cider pressed. It honored the king and queen with feasting and dancing. Symbolically, a sacrifice was made to the Spirit of Vegetation by burning a Wicker Man. This was a human figure made of corn and grain; a practice that might have been added by the Druids. The tales told at that time were about the capture of Persephone.

England celebrated the event with a harvest supper, originally called a "Kern, Mell", or "Horkey Supper". Now it is often a church supper, but in the past, the Lord of the Harvest was honored. He led the scything to clear the fields. The "Lady of the Harvest" was a man dressed as a woman (a stand-in for the Lord.) It was believed that the power of the harvest resided in the last sheaf standing, and an elaborate ritual accompanied felling the last stock, called "John Barleycorn" in the following poem.

There were three men came out of the West,
Their fortunes for to try,
And these three men made a solemn vow,
John Barleycorn must die.

They let him stand till midsummer's day,
Till he looked both pale and wan
And little Sir John's grown a long, long beard
And so became a man...

They've hired men with scythes so sharp,
To cut him off at the knee,
They've rolled him and tied him by the waist
Serving him most barbarously...

And little Sir John in the nut-brown bowl—
And he's brandy in the glass,
And little Sir John in the nut-brown bowl
Proved the strongest man at last.

The Last load in was decorated with branches and garlands and was drawn through the village as everyone rang bells and cheered. People hid in the bushes and threw buckets of water over the cart. (This was imitative magic to insure rain for the next year's crop). The Old Sow (two men in a costume of sacking) appeared, pricking the guests throughout the event.

Farmers provided a good meal for the reapers (and still did when I was growing up in Iowa). Children who helped with the harvest got plum cake to eat. Traditional food for the feast was beef, plum pudding, and beer.

Pilgrims probably brought some of these customs to new world. In 1621, the actual day is not known, but President Lincoln decided that the last Thursday in November would be "Thanksgiving". (In Canada Thanksgiving is in October).

In Rome, this time was the Festival of Dionysus, which was a party that lasted for as many days as followers could remain upright. Dionysus was "God of Vegetation and Wine,"

Ireland, Scotland and Cornwall traditionally visit burial mounds partly to honor females and appease them before Samhain. It was thought that souls could be reabsorbed back into the womb, and only women were allowed in Tir-na-nog, the Land of the Dead. Women adorned the graves while men prepared the feast site. Cemeteries, which were feared the rest of the time, were deemed safe now. Heather and blackberry wine was used for libations.

In the Norse lands, ones Fate was sealed for a year while they fasted and prayed for forgiveness. It was a time for divination and vision quests as well. The always left a few ears of corn in the fields as an offering for Odin's horses, or for "those who dwell under the earth."

Germany celebrated Oktoberfest on the equinox, and this was a major Sabbat for Bavaria. Newswisswein (New White Wine), a milky byproduct was served, sold by glass from crocks (or cauldrons).

The Jews celebrated the Succoth (Feast of the Booths or Tabernacles) because of the command in Deuteronomy; "You shall keep the feast of booths seven days, when you make your ingathering from your threshing floor and your wine press, you shall rejoice in your feast" They had a procession of palm, myrtle, citron and willow branches. Each family built a booth in the garden or on the roof, covered the roof with green boughs and decorated all with produce.

The ancient Mayans also had a harvest celebration, consisting of a turkey meal and ritual ball games and the forest Indians of the American South, the Natchez, had a feast of specially grown corn and ball games.

Arabia interred the last sheaf of grain in a miniature grave with a stone placed at the head and foot, and land owners prayed that Allah would send the 'wheat of the dead'.

At this turn of the year, the Goddess is now the Crone, in her most powerful aspect.

CHAPTER 8

PREPARATION FOR ALL RITUALS

You must create sacred space in which to do your magickal work. Outdoors is great if you have the space, the weather cooperates and you have some privacy, but any space you have will work if properly prepared. It should be clean and uncluttered. Sweep with a broom counterclockwise, saying something like "out all negativity, out!" You can also burn sage or copal, circling counterclockwise.

You will need little bowls for your salt, water, and holy water; a pentacle, which is a physical object inscribed with a pentagram, used as you would a tray; and an athame or first two fingers of your projecting (dominant) hand. I usually do this at the North quarter. Cleanse all tools and things you plan to use with sage, copal or holy water. Set up the altar and quarters with whatever the ritual calls for.

Place the water on a pentacle;
    (receiving hand held up, projecting fingers (or athame) into water)
    Waters pure, untainted by malice
    Life giving fluid drawn from Earth's Chalice
    Blessings pour fourth in Angelic array,

Powers of creation hither display.'

Lift the bowl up with both hands and say: "Mother, be thou adored"

Repeat this process with the salt

Salt divine untouched by hate,
Spirit of life upon earth's slate,
Foundations of honor, held in stealth
Ancient wisdom, manifest wealth.

Lift bowl up with both hands and say "Father, be thou adored"

Add three pinches of the salt to the water,

Visualize the powers combining, as you stir 3x time clockwise, saying:
"Life force combined; blood and flesh,
Water and Earth, as one do we mesh.
This creature most holy doth herein ignite
Calling but good to our sacred rite"

One (or both) people lift up the consecrated water and say;
"Spirit, be thou adored!"

Purify the circle with Holy Water (earth/water):

By salt, which is the body of the Earth, and by water, through which life flows, I do purify and consecrate all this circle may hold. Mother, be thou adored.

Purify Circle with Fire and Air: By the air and fire of creation, I do purify and consecrate all this circle may hold. Father, be thou adored.

Casting the circle

I start in the East. To me, that is the "beginning." Others may start in the North. Go clockwise. You can do this silently, or simply say "I cast this circle 'round about to keep all evil entities out" or whatever works for you. I always use the calls I wrote for myself. Others may do it differently. Again, some choices are personal! Do what feels right to you!

Seal the circle. If you have a group, the person tending the Eastern quarter will go next, sprinkling holy water, circling clockwise around the circle, perhaps saying "I seal this circle with earth and water"

The Western quarter person does the same, but saying "fire and air".

The pentagram is drawn with an athame or your first two fingers. To call a quarter in, step your right foot forward and draw from the element <u>opposite</u> toward the element you are calling in. (For example, If you were calling Air, start drawing from Water.) Step back, kiss the blade of the athame, touch it to your heart (flat) and replace it.

If you are working solitaire, you would just proceed to the next quarter until all four are open.

When each quarter is released at the end of the ritual, step forward and reverse the way you drew the star. (Air – Water – Fire – Spirit – Earth), etc.

Sabbat Rituals (Holy days)

I am including some of the rituals I use. These are usually a composite of things that have been passed down orally, things I've written, things from other covens, historical poems and stories, and probably more. Rituals can also be held for almost any purpose; healing, divination, etc.

RITUALS

SAMHAIN 1: SPIDER WOMAN

https://www.youtube.com/watch?v=1YAShZwKL2g "Enter the Center" (I highly recommend all music by Jeff McBride and Abbie Spinner!

Make holy Water:
> Waters pure, untainted by malice
> Life giving fluid drawn from Earth's Chalice.
> Blessings pour forth in Angelic array
> Powers of creation hither display

Prepare the nine cauldrons:

*1 – 14" strings; one for each person 2 – angel or/divination deck; 3 - "doves blood" (red ink) 4 – fire and flash paper (Epsom salts 1" deep, rubbing alcohol to cover plus 1") flash paper (from magic supply store) 5 – water scented with anointing oil (drum); 6 – hot spiced wine 7 – cakes 8 – charcoal and bowl of incense, 9 –tiny bottles of Lotus Water
CD – "#2, Enter the Center" or other appropriate music, Holy Water
Cast & seal circle*

HPS:
> Black spirits and white,
> Red spirits and gray
> Hearken to the rune I say

Four points of the circle, weave the spell,
East, South, West, North,
Your tale to tell

Three times round the circle's cast
Great ones, spirits from the past
Witness it and guard it fast.

Behold, There is Magick or similar music

EAST

 All hail the Eastern Gate
 From which blows the winds of fate.
 Spirits light, spirits of air
 Dwellers of the red dawn there

 Bring the message here tonight
 From the Fey and from the sprite
 Old ones, guard! Watch if you would
 Evil keep out, admit only good!

SOUTH

 All hail the Southern Gate
 Our courage to raise, our fears abate.
 Spirits of fire, Spirits of Fun
 Dwellers in the white-hot Sun.

 Energy bring and power, too
 For magick old and magick new.
 Old ones, guard! Watch if you would
 Evil keep out, admit only good!

WEST

 All hail the Gate in the West
 Open now at our behest

Spirits of mystery, Water sprite
Twilight gray foretells the night.

Spirits of our loved ones come.
Play the horn and beat the drum.
Old ones, guard! Watch if you would
Evil keep out, admit only good!

NORTH

All hail the Gate in the North
Earthly blessings here come forth.
Earth spirits of wisdom and power
Black spirits of the midnight hour.

Stand fast with us all through this rite
As we honor death's cycle this night.
Old ones guard! Watch if you would
Evil keep out, admit only good!

HPS:

We gather this night of the witches' year end,
To witness the turn of the wheel once again.
To honor our ancestors beyond the veil
Now grown thin as winter prevails.

The Sun king fails, the die has been cast,
The underworld beckons and claims him at last.
Yet the cycle continues and he will return
On the longest, dark night as the Yule fires burn.

Story of Spider Woman: *Speaker #1*

In mythology, the spider is well-known and revered. The Egyptians believed the spider to be an attribute of the Goddess Neith, weaver of the world.

The Chibcha Indians of Colombia believe that the dead cross the Lake of the Dead on boats made of spider webs; they therefore hold the spider in awe and will not kill it.

Other South American Indians believe the spider provides the means of climbing from the Lower World to the Upper World.

Speaker #2
In Greek mythology, the spider is associated with Athena, Persephone, the Fates, the Morai, Harmonia, and Arachne, whom Athena challenged to a spinning contest. Furious because the contest was a tie, Athena slit Arachne's loom and beat her with her shuttle. Arachne was mortified, and so hung herself. Seeing this, Athena sprinkled the body with a magick potion and changed her into a spider.

#1
The spider is prominent in the beliefs of many Native Americans. Myths about spiders vary from tribe to tribe, from village to village, and from storyteller to storyteller.

#2
According to Nauru Island natives, the spider created the world. She birthed herself from the Void. It took a long time, a long, long time. It took eons of time, for She had nothing to work with except the power of Her own thought.

She dreamed Her thought into substance and as soon as She was born She began to spin.

She wove the Sacred Spiral upon which the Universe was born. Stars hung like dew drops on a spider's web in the morn.

As soon as She finished, she traveled back to the center, to the vortex, to the place where She was born, and She began to Dance.

#1

She reminds us to listen to our dreams and to follow our paths, for Grandmother Spider connects to us as we sleep. With her silvery thread, she imparts her wisdom and reminds us to connect to our spiritual sides.

Both:

> O Dark Mother, weaver of the web of the universe,
> Spinner of time and space,
> Come to us with your ancient wisdom!
> Hear our heart songs and heed our pleas.
> Guide us upon your silvery web
> That we be not entangled, but empowered
> By the divine force that connects all life as one!
> So mote it be!

Spider:

> Some of you look upon me with fear, others with loathing,
> Yet I am part of you all—look within, look within!
> Not pretty to see, but powerful beyond measure.
> I, and the "I" in YOU, can create any and all from your thoughts.
> Come into my silver web.
> I am the change that transforms
> I'll spin you a silent silken shroud
> A tomb from which to be reborn!
> I see you cringe and step back
> As you watch my scything jaws
> But before rebirth must come release.
>
> I have created the universe and the stars, the planets,
> the rocks and soil and plants and creatures that fly,
> swim, walk or crawl upon them.

Likewise, the I in YOU, can create your reality: the dreams of your highest vision!

I call to the 9 magickal cauldrons—come forth with the mystery of your cauldrons, that those who are worthy may find the mystery in themselves!

Cauldron #1 – Birth (lengths of ribbon or yarn for each to take) I carry the **Cauldron of Klotho**, first of the three sisters of fate; she who cards and spins the thread of life. She is the womb from which you sprang, and it is by her hand that your life progresses, as it is fated.

> We are what we have been
> Now living once again
> Shadows garnered from the past
> A chance to rectify now at last
>
> Talents, wisdom, victories gained,
> Also in me are contained
> The mystery profound;
> That life goes round and round

(All repeat the last 2 lines as they draw their thread and place it around their necks.)

Cauldron #2 – Divination (angel or other divination cards)
I carry the Cauldron of Lachesis, the weaver of chance; womb of the Goddess, revered by the Bards of old for its wisdom, its magick, and its inspiration. Draw from the realms of magick and see what you need to see.

> Cauldron, reveal that which I seek
> Of the future now you speak.
> An image, a thought, a symbol, a word
> To my sight be transferred.
> To advise of what will be
> That I may walk in harmony.
> (all repeat last 2 lines, tie card to ribbon around neck)

Cauldron #3 – Death (Dove's blood ink)

I carry the **Black Cauldron of Kali**, she who is beyond name or form. Accepting Kali means accepting the reality of physical death. We acknowledge those who have crossed the veil before us with her cauldron. I Anoint your forehead with the blood of your ancestors as you honor and remember them.

All: 'Tis the blood of the ancestors
      That flows through our veins
      The forms change,
      But the circle of life remains

Cauldron #4 – Transformation (fire & flash paper: pass papers) I carry the **Cauldron of Isis**, the Lake of Fire. Only through burning off the dross, can we transform ourselves and be born again anew. Breathe upon this paper a word that symbolizes what you want to transform in yourself or in your life.

      Transform yourself, heal yourself
      What do you wish to change?
      Needs into fulfillment?
      Your shadows to exchange?

      (all repeat)
      I burn this trait now from my life
      Upon this sacred Samhain night
      It is gone from me at last
      Just a memory from the past
      (repeat last 2 lines till done)

Cauldron #5 – Rebirth

(Fill with scented water, sprinkle on top of heads w/rose. Drum heartbeat in the background)

I, Spider Woman, carry the cauldron of **Bran the Blessed** the Cauldron of Rebirth through which life is regenerated and the dead are reborn to live again.

> We all come from the Goddess
> And to Her we shall return
> Like a drop of rain
> Flowing to the ocean
>
> We all come from the Sun God
> And to Him we shall return
> Like a spark of fire
> Rising to the heavens

Cauldron #6 – Wisdom *(play CD: Craicmore #7) (Hot spiced wine and ladle, assisted by tray of cups carrier)*

I carry the **Cauldron of Erda** containing the wise blood stolen from her by Odin. Drink from this and you will obtain wisdom, magick, and cosmic understanding.

Cauldron #7– Plenty CD: Year is a Dancing Woman #4, and cakes to eat

I carry **Undry, Cauldron of Danu**, kept by the Dagda, and from which none walk away in need. Take and eat to insure a never-ending source of plenty in your life.

Cauldron #8 - Fairy: CD: Fairy Heartmagic #10 (Fairy call incense: let each guest put in a pinch breathe deeply.)

As the veil be thin, I carry the **Cauldron of Morrigan**, Queen of the Fairies and all that lies beyond the veil. Breathe the air-borne scent and open your hearts and minds to that which lies beyond.

> Lift the Veil, dare to chance

A glimpse of Samhains Faery Dance!
What lies beyond this mortal coil
Where spirits play whilst we toil?

Dare to see, ask to know
And answers clear are bound to flow
Invite them near and offer a gift
For their assist, the veil to lift!

Cauldron #9 – Fertility *(CD: Fairy Heart Magic: #4, bottles of Lotus Water)*
I carry the Cauldron of Freya, Sea Goddess of fertility, birth and enchantments who brings abundance to the land and to our dreams yet-to-come.

On the next full moon, anoint your belly with this water mixed with Lotus to fertilize your dreams and birth them in the coming spring.

Spider:
These are the mysteries of the cauldron: birth, divination, death, transformation, rebirth, wisdom, abundance, creation, destruction, and regeneration, great magicks all!

And these mysteries are also mine.
I am the Oldest of the old,
Wisest of the wise,
The Power behind power.

I am the light in the dark and the dark of the moon.
I am the One behind the veil, the Threshold to be crossed.
I am the dealer of Death, giver of Rebirth.

I am the greatest of Teachers, with the deepest of lessons.
I am Transition and Connection, the spider in the web.
I am Dusk, Midnight, and the dark before Dawn.
I am Surrender when you need to let go.

I am the Destroyer, and your Protector as well.
I am the One to lead you through the Dark,
through the Fire, into a new day.

I leave you now, but, think of me when you feel pleasure and I
will intensify it—
Until the time when I may have the greatest pleasure,
Of meeting you at the crossroads between the worlds.

Spiral Dance:

> Hand over hand
> Strand by strand
> Thread by thread
> We weave the web

All repeat:

> Farewell, blessed Summer, season of warmth and light
> Welcome to winter, start of a new year, season of dark and cold
>
> Blessed be the New Year
> Blessed be spirit and flesh
> Blessed be the ever-turning wheel
> Blessed be the New Year
> (Throw streamers!)

EAST: Spirits light, spirits of air
Dwellers of the red dawn there
We thank you for the messages you've brought
And for mindfully guarding the Eastern Gate!
Stay if you will, go if you must,
We bid you Hail and Farewell!

North: Earth spirits of wisdom and power
Black spirits of the midnight hour.
We thank you for standing fast with us

And for mindfully guarding the Northern Gate!
Stay if you will, go if you must,
We bid you Hail and Farewell!

West: Spirits of mystery, Water sprite
Twilight gray foretells the night.
We thank you for opening the spirit veil
And for mindfully guarding the Western Gate!
Stay if you will, go if you must,
We bid you Hail and Farewell!

South: Spirits of fire, Spirits of Fun
Dwellers in the white-hot Sun.
We thank you for your energy and power
And for mindfully guarding the Southern Gate!
Stay if you will, go if you must,
We bid you Hail and Farewell! (Open circle).

SAMHAIN 2: THREE FATES

Needs: *Hecate incense, tokens of elements, pieces of paper, pens, spinning wheel, loom, red, white and black candles, triple candle holder, black candles for all, dish of sand, Guide, pendulum, and streamers. CD: born, live, die,*

Cast & seal circle, admit guests

HPS: Black spirits and white,
      Red spirits and gray
      Hearken to the rune I say
      Four points of the circle, weave the spell,
      East, South, West, North, your tale to tell
      Three times round the circle's cast
      Great ones, spirits from the past
      Witness it and guard it fast.

East: All hail the Eastern Gate
      From which blows the winds of fate.
      Spirits light, spirits of air
      Dwellers of the red dawn there
      Bring the message here tonight
      From the Fey and from the sprite
      Old ones guard! Watch if you would
      Evil keep out, admit only good!

South:

> All hail the Southern Gate
> Our courage to raise, our fears abate.
> Spirits of fire, Spirits of Fun
> Dwellers in the white-hot Sun.
> Energy bring and power, too
> For magick old and magick new.
> Old ones guard! Watch if you would
> Evil keep out, admit only good!

West: All hail the Gate in the West
> Open now at our behest
> Spirits of mystery, Water sprite
> Twilight gray foretells the night.
> Spirits of our loved ones come.
> Play the horn and beat the drum.
> Old ones guard! Watch if you would
> Evil keep out, admit only good!

North:

> All hail the Gate in the North
> Earthly blessings here come forth.
> Earth spirits of wisdom and power
> Black spirits of the midnight hour.
> Stand fast with us all through this rite
> As we honor death's cycle this night.
> Old ones guard! Watch if you would
> Evil keep out, admit only good!

Statement of purpose: HPS:

> We gather this night of the witches' year end,
> To witness the turn of the wheel once again.
> To honor our ancestors beyond the veil
> Now grown thin as winter prevails.
> The Sun king fails, the die has been cast,

The underworld beckoned and claimed him at last.
Yet the cycle continues and he will return
On the longest, dark night as the Yule fires burn.

HP *as Dark Lord: (Speaks up from West altar)*

The Sun king is dead and in my domain
Where, until Yule, he must remain.
While in my keep he will slumber and rest
To return as a babe, honored and blest.

*(**HPS** admits Clotho who carries white candle to the altar)*

Clotho: The young year has passed, the light grows thin
Darkness pervades and winter comes in.
The maiden, the youth, the gay light of spring
Withdraws with the sun; now geese on the wing
Trees grow bare, frost nips the ground
Everywhere signs of winter are found.
Keep in your heart the light of the Sun
For he will return before winter is done.
(HPS admits Lachesis who carries red candle to the altar)

Lachesis:
Each night grows longer as daylight recedes;
Each creature retreats, concerned with its needs.
The harvest is in, the cold wind blows
Prepare to prevail through winter's snows.
Will there be food, sustenance for all?
Who will survive through winter's squall?
The God in the underworld, the Crones now rule
The harsh time of winter can be quite cruel.

HPS (as Atropos brings black candle to altar)
The mothers and fathers and children of old

Were strong at heart, courageous and bold
Now is the time to honor our dead
To seek their counsel, to hear what they've said.
For they live on in our thoughts and our heart
Of them you shall always be a part
Their manner of speech, the turn of a head
They live on in you and as so, are not dead.
Celebrate their deeds, the lives that they've led
Remember their souls, the paths that they've tread.

All three: *(join palms up together and circle)*
We are One become Three, each having a part
But joined in the Goddess as one living heart.
Maid, Mother and Crone, One becomes three
Through ancient magicks, the Great Mystery.

(Leave for various rooms)

HP: (at altar)
Turn into the dark, the night of the soul;
Find divine love, which shall make you whole.
Leave regrets behind and all that grieves
Forgive and forget with the fall of the leaves.
Honor the loved and departed ones dear
Greet them with love, with nothing to fear.
And the Gods and Goddesses revere,
For this cycle ends with the Witches New Year.
(Quarters set up chairs, Guide escorts group to Clotho)

HP: The veil is thin this sacred eve
We ask that those for whom we grieve
Come to us in love and peace
Our understanding to increase.
Come with the blessing of Lady and Lord
Come with communication restored.

The door is open, the beacon is lit,
Arise, blessed dead, and with us sit.
(All sit in séance as guides continue to remove groups)

Clotho:

I am Clotho, youngest daughter of Zeus and Themis and Daughter of Night. I spin the thread of your life the day you are born, to be woven into the cloth of your destiny. I am the womb from which you sprang.

Just as the spider spins her patterned web, I've spun your fate – the joys and sorrows you will encounter, the successes and failures, the karma you will bring with you and family you have chosen to be part of.

Choose, that I may inform you of the direction you need take to further your journey along your life's path. (Participant draws a colored tile and Clotho interprets.)

Proceed now to my sister Lachesis.

Lachesis:

I am Lachesis, second daughter of Zeus and Themis and Daughter of Night. I measure the thread of your destiny, therefore determining the length of your life, then I weave the threads into the pattern of your actions. It is by my hand that your life progresses as it is fated. The pattern I weave marks the progress of your soul. Some events are predestined, but some can be altered by chance—by me.

You may ask one question that can be answered 'yes' or 'no'. Write it down and I will give you your answer. Now proceed to my sister Atropos.

Atropos:

I am Atropos, eldest daughter of Zeus and Themis and Daughter of Night. It is I who severs the thread of your life that Clotho spun and

Lachesis measured. I am the tomb, and the womb of rebirth. I am that which is between and beyond this mortal world. I am The Inevitable One and the Inflexible One. I shall choose the manner of your demise, when your time comes to an end, and snip.

Yet as every ending is yet another beginning, the soul survives in the great beyond. There you will be met by loved ones and angels who will guide you and care for you. Many who care are with you always, even in this earthly life. Think of one for whom you mourn. Take this candle to be burned in their honor and return to the temple.

HPS: Bring your candles one by one, place them in the spiraling sand, calling the name of the departed one you have chosen to honor. (CD)

HPS: Ancient Ones, The ground on which we stand, the starter block of our race; the slate on which we write, the pattern behind our lives. You who lived in the times before us, who laid down the way on which we travel, who established traditions that guide our people, whose blood flows red within us, whose genes have engendered us; Dearest Ancestors we are honored by your presence, and feel your love, we now bid you Hail and Farewell.

HP: May these cakes be the essence of the spirit of the father, without which we would not be. Taste the sweetness of rebirth!

HPS: May this wine be the essence of the spirit of the mother, from whom all life flows. Sip the wine of Life!

HP: On this blessed night, we offer our love and gratitude to the triple Goddess, she who gives us life, incarnation after incarnation, and to her consort who waits now in the underworld gathering strength for his return. To our Lord and Lady, we bid Hail and Farewell though we know you are with us always.

East:
> Powers of the East, Almighty Air,

Dwellers of the red dawn there
Giver of inspiration, winds of fate
Thank you for guarding the Eastern Gate.
Stay if you must, go if you will,
We bid you Hail and Farewell

North:

Powers of the North, Almighty Earth.
Fertile Mother, who gave us birth.
Black spirits of the midnight hour
Guarded this gate with wisdom and power.
Stay if you must, go if you will,
We bid you Hail and Farewell.

West:

Powers of the West, Almighty Water,
You warded this gate and did not falter
Spirits of our loved ones came
Through the veil when called by name.
Stay if you must, go if you will,
We bid you Hail and Farewell

South:

Powers of the South, Almighty Fire,
Giver of courage, passion, desire.
Dwellers in the white-hot Sun,
You've held this gate, your work is done.
Stay if you must, go if you will,
We bid you Hail and Farewell

Open Circle

YULE RITUAL 1: YULE LOG

Needs: Red & green altar, Yule log, candles & papers for each, CD: Darkest Night, Red & Green, Didj *music, drum, star/pine incense, 4 quarter tables w/fairy, dragon, mermaid & elf, big iron cauldron, hula hoop*

Cast & Seal circle; I am the Spirit around you, I am divinity within you, I am the light shining through you; I am all that I am!

East: Lord of the East, Light-bringer we call,
On this Solstice eve, darkest of all.
We hopefully await the coming of light
Dispelling the darkness of cold winter's night.
Enlighten our souls, cast out our despair,
For with your light, our shadows repair.
Come to us now on the cold winter wind
Guard us and guide us until this night's end.
So mote it be!

South: Lady of South, Star's-light we call
On this Solstice eve, darkest of all.
The Warmer of Earth is far, far away,
But shall become stronger now with each day.
Fan the light of our spirits held within
Remembering that we are but light within skin.

Come forth from the flames that warm us tonight
Guard us and guide us in all that is right. So mote it be!

West: Sage of the west, Wiseman we call
On this Solstice eve, darkest of all.
Mysterious light of our lady the moon
Help us tonight with our selves to commune.
Bring to us love unconditional and true
That divine love in us awakens anew.
Come forth from ice and moonlit snow
Guard and guide us, *our hearts all aglow.*
So mote it be!

North: Hag of the North, Dark one we call,
On this Solstice eve, darkest of all.
In deepest night ourselves we discover
Our secrets within, our shadows uncover.
But in the dark, Ancient wisdom's revealed
Our pains subside, our souls are healed.
Come forth from the ice cave in which you dwell
To guard us and guide us and help us be well.
So mote it be!

Statement of Purpose:
Yule is the first spoke of the great Wheel of the year. It is the birth of the Divine Child, the Sun God, whose return marks the beginning of the Sun's journey North, bringing its increasing warmth to our Earth. (Light Yule candles)

At Yule, we also honor the power of the longest night of the year and prepare ourselves for the return of the Sun. We turn this power within to purge the shadows that we find there. We seek for the divine, we dream and imagine new possibilities in our lives for the coming year, and determine the qualities that we might bring, like the returning light, into the World.

South: (Step forward)

> This is a time to know the endurance of the land,
> And so to grow in one's own inner strength.
> A time of rest and introspection
> And considering all things.
> It is a season of Renewal...

North: (Step forward)

> This is the time for entering the darkness,
> And seeking its magickal powers,
> A time for standing alone and God-like,
> And seeing all things clearly.
> It is a season of Understanding...

East: (Step forward)

> This is a time for devotion to the way of the Circle
> And seeking the joy of friendship and reunion.
> A time for finding reconciliation,
> Confiding in trusted friends.
> It is a season of Forgiveness and Hope...

West: (Step forward)

> This is the time of seeking
> Both in Nature and within oneself,
> Dreams and visions shall concern the mysteries
> And create results.
> It is a season of dreaming....

HPS:

Quietly, find a comfortable position for our journey into the depths of the dark... please do what you need to be comfortable... Close your eyes and allow your body to relax. Allow your breath to soften and deepen. (Allow time for all to get settled)

CD: Deep in the Darkest Night

Using your breath, send a cord of connection deep into the center of the Earth. Allow that cord to strengthen and deepen with each breath... Feel yourself connecting deeper, and deeper, to the core of the earth... Allow your breath and her breath to become one.

(Begin heartbeat drum, softly, keeping the steady beat through the journey)

Allow your heartbeat to become one with the heartbeat of the Earth...so much of our lives are lived outward, as we speak, and move, and work in the land of brightness. Even at night we surround ourselves with light.

Just for tonight, on this longest night of the year, go inward into the darkness behind your closed eyes, moving into that inner place where all the colors are dark and the darkness is safe and wise.

Behind the darkness of your closed eyes, begin walking on this earth. Feel the weight of your body with each step. Notice the landscape around you, the sky, the plants, and the ground upon which you are walking.

Just ahead of you, you see a dark hole in the ground. Walk to that hole and stand at the edge of it. As you look into the hole, you see a pathway down, that leads to a door. Follow the path downward until you are standing in front of the door. Notice how it looks. It is now time for you to go through it. Press against the door and as you go inward, the door will close softly behind you... shutting out the brightness of the world.

It is dark here, but safe and somehow familiar. You feel warm and protected. You notice a comforting smell... What is it? Allow this comforting darkness to surround and envelope you.

In this safe dark womb, allow yourself to be with your darkness... the places you're afraid to show to the outside world. Allow yourself to love and be with all of your shadows... It is safe to be with them now.

Choose one of the dark places inside you that you want to journey with tonight. What in your life is too heavy to carry any more? It may be a regret, or sorrow, or something you have been unable to forgive yourself for. It may be an emotion, an experience, a memory... It may be a deep pain. It is time for it to be brought to the center.

As we continue our journey to the center, feel with your hands for something to guide you through the darkness. It may be a cord, or a rail; the walls, or a sound. Follow it... It will lead you to the center of the darkness.

You will know you are at the center when you feel her. Even in the darkest dark you can feel what She looks like with your inner eye. She is here to show you what to do with the pain you have brought to her. She is here to show you how to love all of yourself. She has a message for you... You can hear it on the waves of sound.

(didgeridoo music)
Follow the waves of sound deeper and deeper... Allow the waves of sound to carry you to Her.. Hear Her calling to you... Hear her whispers... She is here for you ....

(Journey with the didj... and then a short silence)

Hold your hands out to her. You will feel her place an object in your hands, and as it touches you, it begins to glow. Very faintly at first and then brighter so you can see what it is. It continues to brighten until it feels like you are holding a newborn star in your hands. This newborn light is your love! He is Her gift to you. She is asking you to place Him inside yourself, where you can keep him safe and allow your love to grow. Before we return, ask her any questions you have about your gift....

Thank her for her wisdom and strength and for the beautiful gift you have received...knowing that you can return to her whenever you choose.

Begin to retrace your path... Notice that your path is now being lit by the light that is shining brightly from inside you. See the doorway that brought you here... it is now ajar and a beam of light from the outside world is shining through. As you move towards the door, your eyes adjust to the light from the outside world. Go through the door and travel up the path onto this earth. Feel the weight of your body on the earth. Bring yourself back to this room... back into our circle.

(Drumming stops)

Open your eyes and return to the circle bringing back the light of Trust, remaining in silence.

HPS: (pass candles)

One light awakens the darkness. (light first candle, pass the light to all candles saying;) That light, which symbolizes hope and love, spreads forth into the universe, into our lives, into our hearts. Allow the light of your eyes to connect you with each other. Let your eyes speak for you. (first person saying "I spread the divine light of Spirit")

Enter Mother: (Carrying 'baby' sun and walking doesil)
Mine the tears of joy and grief
Mine the magick of belief.
Mine the earth and mine the sea
And mine, the realm of tragedy.
I hear your hearts as they beat,
I feel the footfalls of your feet,
For I'm the Mother of you all
I'm there to catch you if you fall.
Mine's the gift of food and drink

And the wisdom that you think.

Within my arms, newly born
The Sun returns to light the morn.
The dark recedes more each day,
As he grows strong to light the way.
Greet him now with great good cheer
And give him love throughout the year

(Pass the baby to each participant as they extinguish candles which are collected in cauldron. Each gives a welcome greeting from their hearts, rest chant the following :)

Yule is here the Sun reborn
Pass the wreath and sound the horn
Goddess rests, she's given birth,
Now the Sun gives life to Earth.
And with his birth, one by one
Be reborn, as is the new Sun!

(Play Red & Green spiral dance & pass through the birthing hoop)

Cakes & wine:

HP: (invoke Earth pentagram)
Be this bread the essence of the God, sustenance and seed of all life. I bless this food unto our bodies; bestowing health, wealth, strength, joy and peace, and that fulfillment of love which is perfect happiness!

Eat and be one with the Gods!

HPS: (invoke Earth pentagram)
In these cups be the ecstasy of the spirit and the joy of the Earth. I bless this food unto our bodies; bestowing health, wealth, strength, joy and peace, and that fulfillment of love which is perfect happiness!

Drink and be one with the Gods!

HP: Great Mother, Giver of love and life,
        Accept our gratitude for your presence tonight.
        Thank you for all that you provide, Joy,
        'magick and love, and hope worldwide.
        Through you is the Sun reborn to tonight,
        For you both make our world fertile and bright.
        Keep us and guide us throughout the year
        And teach us to share the light without fear.

East: Lord of the East, bringer of light
        We thank you for guarding our circle this night.
        The light that we seek resides in our hearts,
        But now seen more clearly as darkness departs.
        Our vigil begins and lasts until dawn
        Stay, if you will, till darkness is gone.
        Hail and Farewell!

North: Ancient and Wise, Crone of the North
        Grateful are we that Your wisdom came forth.
        Our shadows we've seen deep down inside
        And know that now here the light will reside.
        Our vigil begins and lasts until dawn
        Stay, if you will, till darkness is gone.
        Hail and Farewell!

West: Wiseman, Sage, Guardian of the West
        We thank you for coming at our behest.
        Your mysteries unfurl like the suns rays at dawn
        And fill us with love and the will to go on.
        Our vigil begins and lasts until dawn
        Stay, if you will, till darkness is gone.
        Hail and Farewell!

South: Lady of South, Warrior and Guard
With us tonight, though the way has been hard.
Showing us light that we carry within
Remembering that we are but light within skin!
Our vigil begins and lasts until dawn.
Stay, if you will, till darkness is gone.
Hail and Farewell!

YULE RITUAL 2: NORSE (GUIDED MEDATATION)

Needs: *Alter, 6 lighters, Yule tree decorated with white lights, libation Bowl, Star for top of Yule tree, altar cloths & decorations, Yule Log, Incense, censer, & charcoal, Candle for Freya, Quarter Candles, Bowl for Holy water, 3 wrapped gift boxes, Chair for Mother Frigga, weapons for Valkyries, Baby doll, markers & basket for ornaments, Cd Player & Cd (Red & Green), cakes and serving tray, Gold glass ornaments, Meade or wine and cups*

HPS: *Cast Circle & Seal Circle with holy water and incense*

Quarter Calls: *(the valkyries enter and run around the circle, swinging their weapons in deosil arcs for a few moments to raise energy before taking their places to call the quarters)*

North:
>Northern wind blow cold, blow clear
>Guardian, we ask your presence here
>Share with us your strength
>On this Solstice night
>Guard the Northern portal
>And nurture our hopes tonight.
>Hail and welcome!

East: Eastern wind blow clean, blow clear
   Guardian, we ask your presence here
   Share with us your wisdom
   On this Solstice night
   Guard the Eastern portal
   And grant us your insight.
   Hail and welcome!

South: Southern wind blow hot, blow clear
   Guardian, we ask your presence here
   Share with us your passion
   On this Solstice night
   Guard the Southern portal
   And guide us with your light.
   Hail and welcome!

West: Western wind blow strong, blow clear
   Guardian, we ask your presence here
   Share with us your cleansing power
   On this Solstice night
   Guard the Western portal
   Let your healing flow through us tonight!
   Hail and welcome!

HP: Statement of purpose:
We gather here tonight to celebrate the Winter Solstice. The wheel continues to turn without beginning and without end. The second half of the year has passed. This time of old was called the Wolf Season, a time of cold and harshness. But surely, as the seasons of warmth shall follow this, so also are our gods with us on this longest night of the year.

HPS: We await the return of the sun. The times that shall come are cold, yet we look to the sky and see the promise of the High Ones: The stars of Freya's gown are high in the winter sky and the Winter Way winds from her feet to mark the path of souls across the sky. So also, in the coldest of seasons is there promise of life and plenty to come.

HP: With the birth of the blessed Sun God, Baldur, the days will once again begin to slowly grow longer.

HPS: We light the Yule log in honor of this joyous season of promise. (HPS & HP light Yule log together)

HPS: Beautiful Freya! Leader of the Wind Riders, thou who weavest fates and destinies…and before whose magicks men and gods do bow… Co-ruler with the Great Odin, of the shining Lands of the Gods…we *call on thee.*

O Freya the Fair One! Be with us here, in this rite to celebrate this joyous night! *(Enter Freya)*

Freya: From the darkness is born the light, from the void, fulfillment emerges. As the time of the Divine Child approaches, what wisdom says the guardian of the North?

North:
>   This is a time to know the endurance of the hills,
>   And to grow in one's own inner firmness
>   A time for scrupulousness and thoroughness
>   And considering all things.
>   It is a season of Confidence!

Freya: As the time of the Divine Child approaches, what wisdom says the guardian of the East?

East: This is a time for entering wilderness,
>   And seeking its magickal strengths.
>   A time for standing alone and godlike,
>   *And seeing all things clearly.*
>   *It is a season for Joy!*

Freya: As the time of the Divine Child approaches, what wisdom says the guardian of the South?

South:

> This is a time of active seeking,
> Both without in Nature and within oneself.
> Eagerness and resolution shall concern mysteries,
> And create results.
> It is a season of Courage!

Freya: As the time of the Divine Child approaches, what wisdom say the guardian of the West?

West:

> This is a time for devotion to the Way of the Wild Places
> And seeking the calmness of solitary locales.
> A time for finding understanding,
> And confiding in trusted friends.
> It is a season of Meditation!

Freya: Thank you, my valkyries… you have offered wise words indeed! Please, all find a comfortable position in which to sit or lie and I will take you on a journey with me.

But before we can begin our journey, you must prepare yourselves. Close your eyes and take a deep, cleansing breath…in through the nose and out through your mouth. Now, as you breath in through your nose, envision the air that you breathe in as a soft, glowing blue-white light. See it and feel it filling your body, flowing through your circulatory system.

As it flows through your body, it collects all tension, stress and negativity, so that as you breathe it out through your mouth, it has turned black. Continue this until you have expelled all the blackened air and your body is completely filled with blue-white light.

(Play CD: deep in the darkest night)

The light feels soothing, comforting. You feel yourself begin to relax, starting at your toes, and slowly progressing upward through your body. Feel your legs relax, then your back. The relaxation spreads out into your arms and hands and up into your neck, until at last it reaches the very top of your head. You are completely and totally relaxed. (Fade music away).

We are standing in the main room of a stone and log house tucked deep in the forest. At the south of this room we see an aged door set into the wall. It is made of heavy wood and is hung with a wreath of holly. We go over to the door and pull on it: the door opens easily and beyond we see snow, trees, and white covered hills in the distance under a late-afternoon Sun. Although we know that the light wind and the snow about our feet must be cold as we step through the door, we still feel warm and comfortable. Each of us is dressed as we deem appropriate for this trek through a world of snow and magic. We pull the door shut behind us, noting that it is set into a small stone hut with a thatched roof.

The trees are lightly powdered with snow and there is the sound of distant wind in the trees. A path leads off to the east, away from the declining Sun, and this we take. The snow crunching under our feet is ankle deep, though sometimes drifting more, sometimes blown away to the bare ground beneath. There is a chill and a bite to the air though the cold does not bother us.

The path leads down into the snowy forest. Overhead low heavy clouds are moving in with the promise of more snow likely. There is the sound of wind in the treetops and somewhere a raven calls in the distance. As we continue along the path, we come upon a meadow. The path leads us through the meadow. At the far edge of the meadow, the path passes beneath a high portal like an inverted 'V', made of two large carven logs. We can't make out any meaning to the angular letters of the strange alphabet carved on the portal, though where the two logs cross near the top the high ends look like stylized hawks or eagles. The last rays of the setting Sun break through the clouds momentarily, and the high gate seems to shine like red gold as we pass through it.

The trail passes through the snow covered underbrush and then into the blue-grey shadows of the forest, with snow flurries whirling down from the dimming sky overhead through the snow covered boughs to either side. The air is sharp and cold, with the scent of evergreen and the delicate touch of occasional snowflakes on our faces.

There is the sound of a bird in the distance, a sort of croaking "caw, caw" that must be from a raven, faint at first, then louder as it approaches. We look up through the snow-flecked dimness to see a dark shadow overhead. The bird obviously sees us and spirals down in our direction in a beating of ebony wings that shakes the snow from the trees all about us so that it falls like a miniature blizzard. The large bird lands next to us. The swirling snow calms and we see that she is perched at about eye-level with us on the broken branch of a dead tree. The raven cocks her head from side to side and looks at us with a quizzical, mischievous expression. We pause for a couple minutes, looking at the bird as she looks back at us. If we are quiet and listen closely, perhaps we can hear in our minds what the Old One has to say. Listen… (Pause for a few moments)

The raven decides that it is time to depart. With a loud raucous "Caw" she spreads her great black wings and beats them powerfully. The snow swirls about us so that we can no longer see the bird, though we can feel the strong wind from her wings, lessening along with the sound of their beating as she flies away. The snowflakes, soft and cold on our faces, settle about us and the raven is gone, though we can hear her call fading over the dark trees, far away.

We continue walking along the snow-covered path. The touch of snowflakes caresses our faces. The wind is fading and the stars are coming out clearly overhead. All is still and silent. Looking up at the sky to the north, we notice what seems like pale curtains of light, shifting and shimmering, glowing in rays and sheets of yellow, blue, red, orange, green, and violet. Patterns that are vague, yet bright, seem almost to crackle in the moonlit sky.

As we reach the top of a hill, we can see that the rippling and changing lights stretch from the horizon to far overhead, spreading to cover the entire northern half of the sky and more. Ahead, just above the horizon, is a single very bright star, and the path points directly to it as we walk on through the swirling snow. We walk down the hill, evergreen forests rising on either side.

We hear the sound of bells, chiming clear in the brisk night air and the distant ring of sleigh bells, soft and musical. The tall pines around us are laced with delicate misting snow and glittering icicles. Sparkles of light glisten here and there in the snow and in the ribbons of ice in the trees, reflecting and refracting every color of the rainbow. The bells are clearer. The lights glistening in the trees become brighter and we realize that they are more than simple reflections of the Moon and the Northern Lights.

We smell wood smoke ahead, and our path breaks out into a good-sized clearing before us. A large half-timbered manor house stands there, its leaded-glass windows shining with the light of candles. Multi-colored jeweled lights sparkle everywhere, even along the flowing curves of the old-style, heavy-shingled roof. The yard before the manor is bustling with activity as a noisy crowd of short, stocky, gnomish men and women hurry about, preparing for what seems to be some sort of celebration. They carry flickering lamps and gaily wrapped packages, talking and laughing. We can hear cheerful singing in the distance. They do not notice us as we walk toward the big house. There are many sleds in the yard with antlered beasts of burden hitched to them.

A figure appears at the doorway of the house, sees us, and waves for us to come over to him. He is a big cheerful man, large and heavy, dressed in brightly-colored, fur-trimmed leathers. His hair and beard are full and white, and when he laughs the windows seem to rattle, so deep and rich is his voice.

He claps us on the shoulders and welcomes us to his place, stepping outside to be with us. He waves toward his many servants, smiling, and says that the place may be rustic, but it's cheerful, warm, and quite a change from his more northern abodes.

The big man looks around with a smile. "I was a god before there were gods," he says, "Yet still, of them all, I am remembered a little." He pauses for a moment and looks off into the light-sparkling distance, wrapped in his own thoughts. He looks back at us with a deep chuckle and reaches down into a gold-trimmed pouch at his belt, then holds something out for us in his big hand. "Here," he says, "I have something for you." We hold out our hands and he puts something into it that tingles and glows bright, warm, and with every color of the rainbow, its light shining even on the glistening trees around us. We look at it and gaze at the bright rainbow light that gives such a feeling of well-being and strength as it rests almost weightlessly in our hands.

He smiles at us through his thick white beard and looks deep within our eyes with his own bright eyes. "Remember," he says. "From the stars you came, and to the stars you shall return. Know full well of your immortality. Keep your sense of wonder and work your life so that you strive for perfection." He waves his big hand over ours and the light settles into each of us, filling us with a feeling of well-being, strength, and wonder as though we could see and know all things. Then it is gone, though we know that his gift is now within each of us.

He says, "Come, I want to show you something." He turns toward the deep, snowy forest where there are lights and sparkles in the trees. He leads us on a path that goes deep within where elf-lights of every color and hue sparkle and glow in and over the trees, within the bushes, and on the snowy ground all around us. The path glistens and glows, sparkling in reds, blues, greens, and yellows. There is thick snow on the ground and in the trees. The place seems warm and filled with power, growing stronger as we walk onward. The air is filled with the sounds of distant bells and music, gentle and soft, like carols we remember hearing years ago.

There is a clearing ahead, and the Ancient King who leads us stops and points at the vast tree, bigger than any redwood, whose base and gnarled roots are before us. Lights and mists are everywhere, as are the sounds of bells, tiny and faint, large and distant. There are scents in the air like incense. The big man points and we see that the roots of the gigantic tree enclose a rustic house, stables and sheds as though they had grown from the tree itself. On closer examination, we see that they are indeed part of the gigantic tree.

The glow is bright as the cheerful, big man leads us on into the house within the tree. There are others here, though they are hard to see: people with features so fine and delicate that they could not possibly be human; beings stocky, massive, and elementally powerful; animals, and creatures of pure colored light. The place radiates strength and power from every wall and nook. The others are going where we are going. Music seems to be everywhere.

We have moved into the structure so that we now seem to be at the very core of the vast tree, where the branches might go forever above us, and the roots forever below. With all the others, seen and unseen, we enter the inner chamber, where the throne is at the center of it all, rough like that which has grown out of the Earth, with a small bed nearby.

The light is bright and the air is perfumed. The Mother is there, she who is at the center of all, holding the new Child in her arms. It seems hard to keep our eyes on the Lady, on the Child, for the light is brilliant, and it seems that vast power rises through the very walls and especially the floors of this rustic place to pervade all. It is as though everything is linked with flowing light that passes into and through us all.

We bow and give greetings to the Great Mother. She smiles, and it is as if a forest suddenly burst into blossom. She looks down at her Child, proud of the new life which has come forth to spread everywhere.

Our bearded friend eases back, and we leave with him. We walk back through this place of elemental power and of life. When we get outside, he shakes our hands and clasps us about our shoulders. "It is time for you to go," he says, "but be sure to come back again, to this, the Source." He points the way for us on the path that glistens off indefinitely into the shimmering and sparkling dimness of the forest. We bid him goodbye and walk away, down the path. As the path goes on, the lights of all colors begin to fade somewhat. The singing and then the bells fade into the soft and peaceful night of the enchanted forest.

We walk on, for how far we are not really certain, and then, abruptly the path ends at a heavy wooden door set into a small stone hut under a small, thatched roof of straw. There is a wreath of holly on the door, and we realize that this is the place from which we started. We push the door open, and see within the room from where we began our journey. We step into the room and push the door shut.

Feel yourself slowly returning to your body, wiggling your fingers and toes, stretching, and when you are ready, open your eyes and move into a standing position.

In your hand you hold the gift from the Ancient King. Charge it now, with your wishes, hopes, and dreams for the coming year and mark it with your initials.

(Odin, Thor, & Loki enter, each carrying a wrapped gift. They walk to where the Mother is seated holding the child near the Yule Tree and one

at a time they bow or kneel before her and place their gift at her feet then depart as a group)

"Ah, I see we have some honored visitors... Wise All-Father Odin, The Mighty Thor, and Loki have come to pay homage to the Mother and Child."

When you have charged your ornament, take it and place it on the tree to be blessed by Mother Frigga and the Divine Child. See how the ornaments shine...like miniature suns. When tonight's festivities are concluded, I bid you each to retrieve your ornament from the tree. Take it home with you and hang it in a place when the sun will shine upon it. Look at it often and remember the gift of the Ancient King. Let it fill you with warmth, hope and peace. May it serve as a reminder that from this night forward, the light will continue to grow brighter, both within and without.

(After everyone has placed their ornament on the tree, Freya will lead the group in a spiral dance to "Red & Green", then direct energy to the tree.)

Cakes & Ale Served at this time.

HPS: Beautiful Freya! Leader of the Wind Riders, Co-rulers with the Great Odin of the shining Lands of the Gods...we thank you for your presence here this Solstice night. Thank you for sharing with us your wisdom and magick. Go if you must, or stay if you will. We now bid you Hail and Farewell!

North: Guardian of the Northern wind
Blowing cold and clear
We thank you for your presence here
Thank you for sharing your strength
On this Solstice night
For guarding the Northern portal,

And nurturing our hopes tonight.
Go if you must or stay if you like.
We now bid you Hail & Farewell!

West: Guardian of the Western wind
Blowing strong and clear
We thank you for your presence here
Thank you for sharing your cleansing power
On this Solstice night
For guarding the Western portal,
And for sharing your healing gifts tonight!
Go if you must or stay if you like.
We now bid you Hail and Farewell!

South: Guardian of the Southern wind blowing hot & clear
We thank you for your presence here
Thank you for sharing your passion
On this Solstice night
For guarding the Southern portal
And guiding us with your light.
Go if you must or stay if you like.
We now bid you Hail & Farewell!

East: Guardian of the Eastern wind blowing clean and clear
We thank you for your presence here
Thank you for sharing your wisdom On this Solstice night,
For guarding the Eastern portal
And granting us your insight.
Go if you must or stay if you like.
We now bid you Hail and Farewell!

Open circle

IMBOLC (IMBOLG)
RITUAL 1: ANGELS

Needs: purple lighting, angel wings, rings, globe, candle crown, candles for all, blue delite (or little tiny light), glow sticks, black lights, or violet flashlight, CD – (Angels, Violet Fire)

Sweep & cleanse circle (Play CD: Angel Invocation as people enter)

Lesser Banishing Ritual of the Pentagram: (vocalize one phrase for each line of the pentagram as you draw it). Start drawing from your left side up to point.)

"Ah –Ta" "Mahl-Koot" "Vih-G'Boo-Rah" "Vih-G'Doo-La" "Lih-Oh-Lahm"

Vocalize "Ah-Men" as you draw the circle around the pentagram

East: Yud-Heh-Vahv-Heh
    Hail Angelic Guardian of the East, Raphael.
    Healer, protector, nourisher of Gaia's children
    Angel of joy, and laughter
    I call thee forth to protect this circle
    And to guard this sacred space.
    So mote it be!

South: Ah-Doh-Nye

>Hail Angelic Guardian of the South, Michael.
>He who brings healing to our world.
>I call thee forth to protect this circle
>And to guard this sacred space.
>So mote it be!

West: Eh-Heh-Yeh

>Hail Angelic Guardian of the West, Gabriel.
>She who brings transformation to the children of mystery
>Angel of resurrection, mercy, and peace.
>I call thee forth to protect this circle
>And to guard this sacred space.
>So mote it be!

North: Ah-Glah

>Hail Angelic Guardian of the North, Uriel.
>He who is the bringer of dreams and prophecy.
>Angel of nature, Psychism, and instruction.
>I call thee forth to protect this circle
>And to guard this sacred space.
>So mote it be!

HP: The Great Wheel of the Year turns now to the time of renewal. As the days lengthen and the sun grows stronger, our thoughts turn to the possibility of new life and new beginnings. Yet it is also a time of peril for many, as new life is fragile; baby animals soon will be born, but not all will survive. New plants begin to stretch toward the light, but not all will reach maturity.

The Angels have long been known as the bringers of light – spiritual light; but they are also so the great protectors of this planet and the life that inhabits it. Tonight we have invoked the angels to ask for their help. We seek to transform ourselves, to help us leave fear and negativity behind, to forgive ourselves and transcend our past and our karma, to become beacons of light for this planet and all its life forms.

To aide us in this process, let us call for the angles and their Queen.

HPS: Brilliant Seraphim to thee we call; circle 'round, bring love to all.

HP: Mighty Cherubim guard our gate; remove from us all sorrow and hate.

HPS: Thrones stand firm, stable be; keep us steady on land or sea.

HP: We call Dominions, leadership true; may we be fair in all we do.

HPS: Circles of protection Powers form; help us weather any storm.

HP: Miraculous Virtues hover near; elemental energies we summon here.

HPS: Principalities bring global reform; bless the world and each babe born.

HP: Glorious Archangels show us the way; To bring peace and harmony every day.

HPS: Guardian angels, with all your might; bless us with your guiding light.

HP: We humbly call to the Angel Queen, come forth tonight, a vision seen.

Queen: *(Switch off overhead lights, approach altar)*

The sphere you see represents the planet Earth. (Shine little flashlight on globe) These rays that shine from my hands symbolize the graces entrusted to me to give to those of our children who ask me for them.

107

The gems from which the rays do not shine (show rings) are the graces of which my children forget to ask.

The light of the angels symbolized their power and presence on earth. Allow me to help you, my children. Seek the light of the angels.

(Light candle crown, South passes out candles to all)

Let these candles symbolize the light of love and peace. Let these candles kindle the light within your souls. Let these candles be a beacon to those who love and protect you, to be with you in trying times and in good times. Let these candles stand for the light that joins and unites all life!!!!

(Play CD while all light their candles from the crown, then are placed on respective altars. Queen departs?)

HPS: The violet flame is the essence of a unique spiritual energy; conjured by alchemists of old, who knew that to transmute matter, they must first transform themselves. It is the highest visible light frequency; the point of transition to the next octave of light. It is carried by angels for it can heal emotional and physical problems and will assist the spiritual growth of mankind.

This light, this violet flame was released to the world earlier this century by the Ascended Masters to aid the growth and transition of beings on this planet. This spiritual fire can change inharmonious thoughts and feelings; stress, anger, depression; into a positive and centered disposition.

The Violet Flame will cleanse your system of emotional and physical poisons. It will transmute karma. It will erase the cause behind the effect of disease. It will even clean the distressing records of past lives. Come forth as you feel called. Bathe in the violet light. Ask for the healing it can give, and give your gratitude in return.

(CD: Violet Flame)

(HP & HPS anoint & give gift)

HP: Let this food of the Gods be blessed with his gifts; pleasure, protection, courage and strength. Eat and be blessed by the Gods.

HPS: Let this fruit of the vine be blessed with the gifts of the Goddess; compassion, connection, wisdom and love. Drink and be blessed by the Goddess.

HP & HPS in turn:

Brilliant Seraphim who came to our call; and circled with love for all.

Mighty Cherubim who guarded our gate; removed from us all sorrow and hate.

Thrones stood firm and stable, and kept us steady and able

Dominions called, leadership true; keep us fair in all that we do.

Circles of protected, Powers formed to help us weather any storm.

Miraculous Virtues hovered near; elemental energies we summoned here.

Principalities bring global reform; bless the world and each babe born.

Glorious Archangels show us the way; bringing peace and harmony every day.

Guardian angels, as you might; please bless us with your guiding light.

We humbly thank the Angel Queen, who came forth, a vision seen.

Departing now to your lovely abode, blessings upon us you bestowed.

We invite you to stay, though you're always near, and celebrate with us in good cheer.

So mote it be!

HP: Remember, your guardian angels are always with you, in you and through you.

HPS: Remember that YOU are the light! Carry and spread that light each moment of your life, for it is your charge to bring light into this world.

East: Raphael, Guardian of the East,
      Angelic being who brings the breath of life
      And powers of light,
      Our gratitude now flows to you.
      Thank you for guarding this circle and
      Assisting us with this healing rite.
      Stay if you will, go if you must,
      Hail and Farewell.

North: Uriel, Guardian of the North
      Angel of the throne
      And powers of law
      Our gratitude now flows to you.
      Thank you for guarding this circle and
      Assisting us with this healing rite.
      Stay if you will, go if you must,
      Hail and Farewell.

West: Gabriel, Guardian of the West,
      Angel of the waters of grace
      And the powers of life.
      Our gratitude now flows to you.
      Thank you for guarding this circle and

Assisting us with this healing rite.
Stay if you will, go if you must,
Hail and Farewell.

South: Michael, Guardian of the South,
Angel of the Solar rays
And powers of love,
Our gratitude now flows to you.
Thank you for guarding this circle and
Assisting us with this healing rite.
Stay if you will, go if you must,
Hail and Farewell.

Open Circle

IMBOLC (IMBOLG) RITUAL #2: RETURNING LIGHT

Needs: *seeds in small cups for all, oil lamp, God/Goddess candles, tea lights for all, anointing oil, candle holders, pitcher of milk/honey, cups to pour into, holly crown, circlet.*

Cast & seal the circle

HPS: We are between the worlds, where there is no time, where birth and death, night and day, dark and light are all one.

East: O Air, I call to the Eastern tower.
       Stir fresh new winds of mental power.
       Sweep clear our minds of past debris
       Blow forth new thoughts of clarity.
       Guardian of the Eastern sphere
       Now we seek your presence here.
       Come, East, Come! Be here this night.

South: O Fire, I call to the Southern tower.
       Burn bright the flames of spirit power
       Charge us with your energy,
       Inspired will and intensity.
       Guardian of the Southern sphere

Now we seek your presence here.
Come, South, Come! Be here this night.

West: O Water, I call to the Western tower.
Wash our souls with waves of power
Cleanse and heal us, let us know
Our path of truth within your flow.
Guardian of the Western sphere
Now we seek your presence here.
Come, West, Come! Be here this night.

North: O Earth, I call to the Northern tower.
Protect us with your strength and power.
As your seedling sprout, we see and know
How our new plans must form and grow.
Guardian of the Northern sphere
Now we seek your presence here.
Come, North, Come! Be here this night.

HPS: I greet you all in the name of the Goddess, be She Brigit, Artemis, Diana, Athena, Gaia or another of her many names. She is Maid and Mother and Crone, and tonight we look upon her young beautiful face as she awaits her lover, the God in his youthful glory. (light candle)

HP: I greet you all in the name of the God, be He Pan, Apollo, Horus, Lord of the Forest or another of his many names. He is Youth and Father and Shaman, and tonight we see Him in His prime, strong and sure as He proclaims His love. (light candle)

Both: Together they bless us. We are in the presence of the Divine.

Statement of Purpose: HPS

Tonight we celebrate the Festival of Light. Daylight is increasing and the time for planting comes near. Humans and animals begin to move once more out of their homes, and the slow languid pace of winter energy reluctantly gives way to spring's more rapid pace.

Holly King, Winter King, you who embody the vibrant energy of God within, I call your spirit to this rite. Fill this, your priest, with light and through him shine; to touch your light and kindle hope within us all. As it is willed, so mote it be. (place holly crown on HP)

HP: O bright Goddess of Fire and inspiration, hopes are high in this season, but incomplete without you. O Mother of life, who called me forth from the darkness, I now call you to this celebration of increased light. Fill this, your priestess with the wisdom of your spirit, and through her touch the Goddess within us all. As it is willed, so mote it be. (place circlet on HPS)

HPS: I call the Lord of Light! You were Sun reborn at Yule, now come forth with the bright hopes of youth. (young Lord steps to the altar)

So here we are once again, my Son, in the earliest months of your new cycle of growth. Quite a difference I see already. Your youthful energy already begins to warm me with the promise of spring. Your light grows stronger with each passing day.

Lord of Light:

Yes, I've been having fun since Yule, shining brightly every day, but try as I might, I don't see anything happening yet. I thought I'd set the world on fire, and I can't even make winter go away.

HPS: Have patience, Son. The wheel turns slowly. Spring will come soon enough. I can see you grow with each passing day, even if you're not so sure just yet. We can all help. Let's call the power of fire.

All 3: We call the power of fire with fire to magickally aid the sun's increase. *(light oil lamp)*

HPS: Humans owe their very existence to fire; from the sun's fire that warms the planet to the smallest candle flame that lights the path. How fitting then, that we celebrate the return of the sun's fire by lighting candles to show our hope and faith in that return. Together we are going to anoint and charge a candle to burn for our festival and our intentions. Come forth, young maiden, join us in our celebration of the returning light. *(enter maiden)* The Maiden will now bring the basket of candles to you; please take one. *(pass out candles)*

HP: The Crone bears a container of oil spiced with myrrh and cinnamon. The oil is a symbol of fertility, being the seed of the tree, and cinnamon is for success, protection and love. Myrrh is also for protection, as well as healing and spirituality. As we share the oil, you will charge your candle with your hopes for the coming seasons. Picture the positive results from the changes you first spoke of at Yule, or the results from your own desires for change within your life at this time—weight loss, ending addictions, a more positive outlook on life, whatever it is that you want to change.

HPS: Rub the oil on your candle clockwise as you see in your mind the end results of your wish. This is the time to build the light. It is the time when the darkness, the past, must be banished. Let go, so that the visions, ideals and goals may now crystallize into visible form for each of you. As you see it in your mind, know that you are making it so. If you believe something, you will act on it. Believe that you can make these changes!

Crone: At Samhain I, the Crone, became the Watcher of the Fire. It is time for me to relinquish my duties to the young Maiden. Let the one who tends the fire be given the visions. (Maiden comes forth to receive the fire.)

Maiden: *(CD – Return of the Sun)*

I will tend the fire and I welcome the visions.

(Bow to the Crone and take the flame to each person)

I give you my fire. May it burn away the past and bring light into your future.

(When all are lit) This spark that we share us is but a small symbol of the Divine; our way of acknowledging the Universal Fire that burns in all that is. *(Maiden and young lord retire)*

HP: I stand in the presence of the Divine Light, that sacred spark that is each and every one of us. Winter ends, spring returns. The seeds of greatness are planted and will come to fruition in their own time. Change is inevitable and I welcome that change as a reminder of my own possibilities. I came from the light, brought forth as a Divine being to experience and learn all that life will teach me. I am the light, a spark to help others through the darkness. I will be the light, passed like a candle from person to person to destroy negativity and to create positive energy in the Universe, where everything is interconnected, to come around again to the beginning.

Please repeat after me as you gaze into your candle:

> *I came from the light.*
> *I came to learn.*
> *I am the light.*
> *I help others through the darkness.*
> *I will be the light.*
> *I grow and change to become ever more sacred.*

Please place your candles on the altar.

All: *Winter Goes, Sunlight grows, Fire burns, spring returns*

(repeat 3 times).

HPS: Be comfortable now, and prepare for our meditation.

Breathe in. Breathe out.

Close your eyes and see these pictures in your mind. There is an open space in the forest, a clearing of sorts. Trees ring this area, where the dirt is dark and moist, ready to receive any seeds it may nourish. You are that seed, carried by a bird and dropping into the space, pushed into the welcoming loam by a deer's foot, tamped into place and waiting in the dark.

Breathe in. Breathe out.

You can feel the dirt around you, feel the earthworms as they aerate the soil and provide fertilizer, food for you to grow. You are even vaguely aware of the heat of the sun, shining down from above, warming the land. Sometimes you are cooled by the gentle trickle of rain as it soaks into the dirt. You exist, only exist; a seed in the dark, warm nourishing body of the Mother. Time passes and you begin to feel...different.

Breathe in. Breathe out.

Your insides move, spin, feel...odd. Your seed hull begins to feel tight, like it's gotten smaller. The worms do their job, the sun shines and the rain falls. You expand, pushing against the hull, breaking free with a tendril that pokes up in the dirt, reaching for Father Sky.

Breathe in. Breathe out.

You continue to grow, sending little rootlets out into the dirt to gather the food your body needs to continue seeking the light. The main stem, once that little tendril, now thicker and larger, keeps growing up, pushing through the soil until you suddenly pop! Out into the sunshine. The feel of the sun on your stem causes other changes. Your roots have to grow bigger because now you are sending out leaves. The first two are baby leaves, round and near the soil. You feel them unfurl, soaking up the sun's energy and fueling you with the strength to grow even more, putting out more leaves.

Breathe in. Breathe out.

Your stem thickens, becomes a trunk. You grow more, branches spreading out above as your roots grow down, digging deep into the rich dirt, pulling nourishment from the darkness as your leaves reach up to the sun, pulling nourishment from the very light that strikes them. You are aware of other life around you: other trees, other plants. You are large enough that the small animals have begun to live in your branches and around your roots.

Breathe in. Breathe out.

You welcome the birds, the squirrels, the chipmunks that scamper up your trunk. You nestle your roots around the rabbit's den and gently cradle the opossum in your branches. The winds blow and your leaves dance wildly in the stream of air; the rains come and the water pours onto your leaves, down your trunk and soak the ground. The seasons change; your leaves die and fall off only to grow again in the next spring. A woodpecker drills a hole in your side and you grow a protective covering. The opening that is left becomes a safe home for small animals.

Breathe in. Breathe out.

The snows of winter blanket you and you sleep through the cold. The warmth of spring stirs the core of your being and you grow again, through summer's abundance and into fall's chill, year after year, season after season. You send out seeds of your own, dropped on the ground or carried off by birds. Some of them will grow, some will not but it doesn't matter to you, you just keep making seeds and sending them out into the world. Your roots grow down and out into the dark soil as far as your branches and leaves grow up and out into the light. You can feel all that is around you; the other trees, other plants, the animals, the bugs, everything that lives and breathes and grows, all of it connected in the delicate waltz of life; taking energy, giving energy, living and dying and living again.

Breathe in. Breathe out.

Slowly, at your own pace, allow yourself to hear, to be aware of, the other people here. Be aware of the ones here in this space as well as other people in the building. Be aware of the people on the street outside. Be aware of the people who are in this town...in this state...in this country...on this planet.

Breathe in. Breathe out.

Come back into this space when you are ready, and open your eyes.

HP: Before you are some seeds. Take them up and charge them with your energy. Think upon the things you would cast into the world, hoping that they take root and grow. Charge them with magickal intent, that they may heal this planet and fill its people with positive energy, health and hope, well-being and inner peace; equip the people of the Earth with the tools to withstand, accept and cope with whatever comes to them.

HPS: When I give the call, cast the seeds toward the altar!
> This magick we weave
> For Earth, our mother
> For peace and hope
> For each sister and brother.
> For Mother Earth,
> And her creatures all,
> We thank and bless
> Let the seeds **now fall!**

HPS: We are a circle—We are an eclectic circle—No one path is the only way and we encourage the seeking of alternate routes. We are all students—Each person can learn more than they know today. We are all teachers—Each person has lessons to share. We are a resource to each other and to the community at large—We share what we have and what we know and what we can do. We are a spiritual group that celebrates our beliefs through shared ritual observances—We know that all acts of love and pleasure are acts of worship. We are magickal beings who can create wondrous things—We work together to improve our world, always mindful of the three-fold law.

Wine & Cakes: *(HSP with chalice of milk & honey, HP with athame)*

HPS: Athame to Cup
    HP: Sword to Chalice

HPS: Lance to Grail
    HP: Man to Woman

HPS: God to Goddess
    HP/HPs Conjoined, they bring blessedness to life.
    (Pour Milk & Honey)

HP: May you never thirst my Lady.
    HPS: May you never thirst my Lord.

HP & HPS: *(To all)* May you never thirst!

HP & HPs: May these cakes be blessed with all things needed for life.

(pass cakes)

HPS: May you never hunger my Lord.
    HP: May you never hunger my Lady.

HP & HPS: *(To all)* May you never hunger!

HP: We thank the Maiden who has given us her fire and her blessings, and look forward to the fertile spring.

HPS: We thank the young Lord of Light, who has come to share his light with the world. We look forward to the fertile spring.

HP: Mother of Life, of fire and inspiration, we do thank you for your love and care. Stay if you will, go if you must, we bid you Hail and Farewell.

HPS: Holly King, bright Lord who embodies the vibrant energy of the God within, we do thank you for your strength and love. Stay if you will, go if you must, we bid you Hail and Farewell.

East: You've swept away our past debris
      And brought fresh winds of clarity
      Power of Air, our thanks to thee
      Stay if you will, go if you must
      Hail, farewell, and Blessed be

North: As seedlings sprout, we'll see and know
      How our new plans must form and grow.
      Power of Earth, our thanks to thee
      Stay if you will, go if you must
      Hail, farewell, and Blessed be

West: *You've cleansed, healed, and helped us know*
      Our path of truth, within your flow.
      Power of Water, our thanks to thee
      Stay if you will, go if you must
      Hail, farewell, and Blessed be

South: *You've charges us with your energy,*
      Inspired will and intensity.
      Power of Fire, our thanks to thee
      Stay if you will, go if you must
      Hail, farewell, and Blessed be

CLOSE CIRCLE

OESTARA RITUAL 1: THE KALEVALA

Needs: *nest, eggs, big egg, birds & eggs at quarters, seeds, drums, Eros & Aphrodite, Goddess & God candles*

On altar: *Lily, basket of eggs, fairy, God/Goddess statues, wheel, besom(broom), incense-charcoal-censor-lighter, feather fan, sword/athame, candles, salt-water-bowl, wine-cups-tray, libation bowl, donation box, stand-script-light.*

Cast and seal circle

East: Now comes the turn of the Wheel to Spring,
    Felt within each living thing
    As breezes replace winter gales
    And warmer temperatures prevail.

    New life springs forth on every hand
    And verdant green covers the land.
    Our thoughts turn now to life anew
    Begin again, the old eschew.
    East winds guard this portal fast
    The sacred circle now is cast!
    So mote it be!

South: Now comes the turn of the Wheel to Spring
　　　　Felt within each living thing.
　　　　As daylight grows and shadows fade
　　　　White clouds across blue skies parade.
　　　　Warming sun brings life's return
　　　　And in all species, desires burn
　　　　For the miracle to occur
　　　　To one's nature all defer.
　　　　Southern Fire, guard this portal fast
　　　　The sacred circle now is cast!
　　　　So mote it be!

West: Now comes the turn of the Wheel to Spring
　　　　Felt within each living thing.
　　　　Winter's ice and snow-melt goes,
　　　　To rushing streams and lakes it flows.

　　　　From seeming death comes life resurrected;
　　　　Held in the womb of the Goddess protected.
　　　　Birthed now in the gentle rains of spring
　　　　Comes forth every new and fragile thing.
　　　　Waters of the West, guard this portal fast
　　　　The sacred circle now is cast!
　　　　So mote it be!

North:
　　　　Now comes the turn of the Wheel to Spring
　　　　Felt within each living thing
　　　　The spark of life within each seed,
　　　　Within each species finds a need
　　　　To reproduce, to procreate
　　　　To bring forth life, strong and straight
　　　　With hope and love and joy springs forth
　　　　As winter flees to the North.
　　　　Mother Earth, guard this portal fast

The sacred circle now is cast!
So mote it be!

Statement of Purpose: HPS:

On the Spring Equinox, we stand at the perfect balance of light and dark; the perfect balance of feminine and masculine, God and Goddess. Past that singular point in time, the light steadily grows stronger and spring warms into summer.

HP: For thousands of years, the resurrection of life at springtime has been symbolized, celebrated and personified in mythology with the many stories of slain Gods and Saviors. But with the increasing light, the trees and plants of this world also come to life, resurrected from winter's dark, cold grip.

It is the time of the maiden, who represents the spring. It is also the time of new beginnings, love and fertility, for the cycle could not continue without the union of the God and Goddess. All would be barren and dead; all flora and fauna would cease to be without love and desire.

HPS: One of the symbols of fertility, and even creation, has become common place at this time of the year – the egg!

In the mythology of many cultures, the egg is the vehicle through which the world was created. One Egyptian story of creation is that the Chaos Goose and the Chaos Gander produced an egg that was the sun, Ra. The gander was Geb, the earth god.

HP: Chinese myths say that in the beginning there was darkness everywhere, and Chaos ruled. Within the darkness there formed an egg, and inside the egg the giant Pangu came into being. For aeons Pangu slept and grew. When he had grown to gigantic size he stretched his huge limbs and in so doing broke the egg. The lighter parts of the egg floated upwards to form the heavens and the denser parts sank downwards, to become the earth. And so was formed earth and sky, Yin and Yang.

HPS: The myth of the Dogon tribe, whose knowledge of astronomy astounded the explorers who discovered them, also refers to the cosmic egg. The creation deity begins the act of creation by placing two embryonic sets of twins in an egg, each set being a male and a female. During the maturation process they merge together thus forming androgynous beings.

HP: In a Tahitian myth, the creator deity himself lives alone in a shell. After breaking out of the shell, he creates his counterpart, and together they undertake the work of creation.

HPS: The Hindu texts known as the Upanishads describe the creation of the world as the breaking of a cosmic egg. For the Greeks, there existed only the empty darkness and a Nyx, a bird with black wings, who laid golden eggs, but this myth seems to be related to the mythology of the Finns.

HP: In Finland the pagan tradition has remained unbroken. Their mythology, which was passed down by oral tradition for many generations, was finally written down in the 19th Century. It is from this epic work, the Kalevala, that much of Tolkien's" Lord of the Rings" was taken.

The Myth:
HPS: In primeval times, a maiden, Beauteous Daughter of the Ether,

Passed for ages her existence in the great expanse of heaven, O'er the prairies yet enfolded.

Wearisome the maiden growing, Her existence sad and hopeless. Thus alone to live for ages in the infinite expanses of the air above the sea-foam, In the far outstretching spaces, in a solitude of ether.

She descended to the ocean, waves her coach, and waves her pillow. With her play the storm-wind forces, On the blue back of the waters; On the white-wreathed waves of ocean, Play the forces of the salt-sea, With the lone and helpless maiden; Till at last in full conception, Union now of force and beauty, Sink the storm-winds into slumber;

HP: Overburdened now the maiden, Cannot rise above the surface;

Seven hundred years she wandered, Ages nine of man's existence, Swam the ocean hither, thither, Could not rise above the waters, Conscious only of her travail; Seven hundred years she labored Ere her first-born was delivered.

Thus she swam as water-mother, toward the east, and also southward, toward the west, and also northward; Swam the sea in all directions, Frightened at the strife of storm-winds, Swam in travail, swam unceasing, Ere her first-born was delivered. Then began she gently weeping, spake these measures, heavy-hearted:

Water-Mother (HPS)
Ukko, thou O God, up yonder, Thou the ruler of the heavens,

Come thou hither, thou art needed, Come thou hither, I implore thee,

To deliver me from trouble, To deliver me in travail.

Come I pray thee, hither hasten, Hasten more that thou art needed,

Haste and help this helpless maiden!

HP: When she ceased her supplications, scarce a moment onward passes, Ere a beauteous teal descending, Hastens toward the water-mother, Comes a-flying hither, thither, Seeks herself a place for nesting.

Flies she eastward, flies she westward, Circles northward, circles southward, Cannot find a grassy hillock, Not the smallest bit of verdure;

Cannot find a spot protected, Cannot find a place befitting, Where to make her nest in safety. Flying slowly, looking round her, she descries no place for resting, Thinking loud and long debating, and her words are such as follow:

Teal: Build I in the winds my dwelling, on the floods my place of nesting? Surely would the winds destroy it; far away the waves would wash it.

HP: Then the daughter of the Ether, Now the hapless water-mother,

Raised her shoulders out of water, Raised her knees above the ocean,

That the teal might build her dwelling, Build her nesting-place in safety.

Thereupon the teal in beauty, flying slowly, looking round her,

Spies the shoulders of the maiden, Sees the knees of Ether's daughter,

Now the hapless water-mother, Thinks them to be grassy hillocks,

On the blue back of the ocean.

Thence she flies and hovers slowly, Lightly on the knee she settles,

Finds a nesting-place befitting, Where to lay her eggs in safety.

Here she builds her humble dwelling (place nest on HPS knees.)

Lays her eggs within, at pleasure, Six, the golden eggs she lays there, (putting in eggs)

Then a seventh, an egg of iron; Sits upon her eggs to hatch them, (place bird)

Quickly warms them on the knee-cap Of the hapless water-mother;

Hatches one day, then a second, Then a third day sits and hatches.

Reader: Warmer grows the water round her, Warmer is her bed in ocean, While her knee with fire is kindled, And her shoulders too are burning, Fire in every vein is coursing.

Quick the maiden moves her shoulders, Shakes her members in succession, Shakes the nest from its foundation, and the eggs fall into ocean, Dash in pieces on the bottom of the deep and boundless waters.

In the sand they do not perish, not the pieces in the ocean; But transformed, in wondrous beauty all the fragments come together (show big egg) Forming pieces two in number, one the upper, one the lower, Equal to the one, the other. From one half the egg, the lower, Grows the nether vault of Terra: From the upper half remaining, grows the upper vault of Heaven.

HP: From the white part come the moonbeams, From the yellow part the sunshine, From the motley part the starlight, From the dark part grows the cloudage; And the days speed onward swiftly, Quickly do the years fly over, From the shining of the new sun, From the lighting of the full moon.

Thus ends the story of creation from the Kalevala.

HP:

During the dark months, we have carefully planted our seeds of intent, and we stand now at the point of equilibrium between the past and the future. Now it is time to tend the garden—to take the action that will bring us closer to our dreams and goals. Just as life cannot stand still and the only constant in this world that we know is change, we must also spring forward. If we do not, we will surely fall back, repeating our past mistakes and reaping our dissatisfaction.

HPS: *(pass out plastic eggs)*

These eggs are the symbol of the Goddess, the divine feminine, fertility, the ability to create life. As the world begins to create the new cycle of life in the Spring, it is also time for us to actively engage in the creative process that will bring us to our goals. Just as the process of growing life begins when the egg is fertilized, we make a commitment to put our energy into the realization of our dreams. I invite you to place your intention of that dream inside your egg now. *(All charge their eggs)*

HP: This seed is the symbol of the God, the divine masculine and new beginnings, of growth toward harvest—the beginning of the process that will bring your wishes, dreams and desires to fruition. It symbolizes the steps which you must now take and the energy you must expend to make these desires into realities. *(Puts seed in each egg, which then become rattles)*

All Chant: *(drums)*
> Seed and egg, egg and seed,
> Bring to us the things we need.

HPS: The seed is planted and life grows anew in the womb of the Goddess and in our hearts, minds, and material manifestation. An it harm none so mote it be.

HPS: Bless this spiritual food unto our bodies bestowing upon us health, wealth, strength, peace, and the perfect fulfillment of love that is perfect happiness. In these eggs be the promise of ever-renewing life. Eat and be one with the Gods!

HP: Bless this spiritual food unto our bodies bestowing upon us health, wealth, strength, peace, and the perfect fulfillment of love that is perfect happiness. In this wine be the promise of the harvest yet to come. Eat and be one with the Gods!

East: East winds, we thank you for guarding the portal of the East. We look forward to your gentle spring breezes and the new beginnings in the world and in each of us. Stay if you must, go if you will, hale and farewell.

North: Earth Mother, we thank you for guarding the portal of the North. We look forward to the appearance of budding leaves, flowers and new life that signal the growing season begins. Stay if you must, go if you will, hale and farewell.

West: Waters of the West, we thank you for guarding the portal of the West. We look forward to the gentle rains that bring life to the forests and fields and to all that lives. Stay if you must, go if you will, hale and farewell.

South: Southern Fire, we thank you for guarding the portal of the South. We look forward to longer warmer days, to be in nature in our work and play. Stay if you must, go if you will, hale and farewell.

Open Circle

OSTARA RITUAL 2: DEMETER AND PERSEPHONE

On altar: *Lily, basket of eggs, fairy, God/Goddess statue, wheel, besom incense/charcoal/censor/lighter, feather fan, sword/athame, candles, salt/water/bowl, wine/cups/tray, libation bowl, donation box, stand/script/light,*

Sweep circle counter-clockwise to expel any negativity and prepare Holy Water.

Purify Circle with Earth & Water then by Fire and Air.

Call quarters 'Behold there is Magick'

EAST

By the air which is her breath,
Guardians of the East
Spirits of Air, come,
By the Wand
I call thee!
Wisdom and knowledge, Life and Breath
Winds of change,
Winged Fairies,
Send your essence, Come! Be with us now!

SOUTH

By the Fire which is her spirit
Guardians of the South,
Spirits of Fire, come,
By the Sword I call thee!
Passion and flame, Life and will,
Desert dancer,
Dragon of noontide
Send your essence, Come! Be with us now!

WEST

By the Water which is her blood
Guardians of the West,
Spirits of Water, come,
By the Chalice I call thee!
Healing and pleasure, happiness and Love
Mystery of Mysteries
Undines and Sprites
Send your essence, Come! Be with us now!

NORTH

By the Earth which is her body,
Guardians of the North
Spirits of Earth, Come,
By the Pentacle I call thee!
Strength and Wisdom, Prosperity and Growth,
Dark caverns,
Gnomes of Earth
Send your essence, Come! Be with us now!

HPS: Hear ye now the words of the Star Goddess; She in the dust of whose feet are the Hosts of Heaven, whose body encircleth the universe:

I who am the beauty of the green earth
And the white moon amongst the stars,

133

And the Mystery of the waters,
And the desire of the hearts of men, call unto thy soul.
Arise and come unto Me.
For I am the soul of nature who giveth life to the universe.
From Me all things proceed
And unto Me all things must return.
And behold my face, beloved of Gods and men.
Thine inmost divine self shall be enfolded in the rapture of the infinite.
Let My worship be in the heart that rejoices:
For behold, all acts of love and pleasure are my rituals.

Behold, the Lord and Lady of life and the givers of life.
Without her Lord, the Goddess is barren
Without his Lady, the Lord has no life.
Each is needful of the other for completion and power,
As Sun to Earth the spear to the cauldron
Spirit to flesh, human to human.

READER:

The wheel turns—the seasons change, the light and the dark dance with each other in an unending rhythm. The dark, long cold days of Winter have given way to the lengthening days of light on this, the vernal equinox. Spring is coming to the land, and from the death of Winter springs new life.

It is the resurrection of the dance of life! The dance of sprouting seeds and flowing sap as the growing things begin anew. It is the season of creation. The Earth is caressed by the loving touch of the Mother and the land becomes fertile again. Where her hand passes, buds burst open. Leaves and grasses and vines unfurl. She creates a vision of green beauty, so breath-taking after the dark solitude of Winter.

It is this vision that we celebrate on Ostara—the resurrection of life, the world recreating itself—-the returning from the death of winter into the new life of Spring, through the love of the Lord and Lady.

DEMETER/PERSEPHONE Skit

Demeter:

I am Demeter, the Eternal Mother, Corn Goddess and Mistress of Magick. It is I who gave the first wheat seeds to humans. I taught them how to cultivate the soil and plant the grain. It is I who taught them how to make bread from the grain at harvest time. It is by my magick that a bountiful harvest is insured.

My heart is heavy. I have been searching for my daughter, Persephone for many days. This is unlike her. She always returns from enjoying the flowers and the vines and fruits of my labors. I am full of sorrow! Have you seen her? Have you? I have searched the four corners of the world, yet she is not to be found.

Helios, I see that you are about to embark on your journey across the sky, but stay a moment. Have you seen my daughter Persephone?

Woe! Woe, Hades? No, I cannot bear it! Until she is returned to me, I shall curse the land!

Winds of the East—blow strong and cold, that the seeds of the field lay sleeping until my daughter is returned to the Land of the Living!

Light of the South—weaken! Grow distant and dim! Withhold your energy that growth be suspended!

Waters of the West—come forth in icy crystals that no longer quench the thirst of the parched land.

Earth Mother of the North—slow the sap of the trees and hold the sleeping seeds in your dark, cold bosom that they may not sprout and grow.

Zeus, do you hear? What offerings will you receive from your farmers now?

All: Zeus, Great Lord of the Heavens, we beseech you. Our fields lie fallow, our orchards are bare, our flocks suffer from hunger and game is no longer plentiful in the forests. Without your help all will perish. Zeus, protector of the weak and dispenser of Justice, we beg your assistance.

Hermes to Hades: Hades, I come from Zeus. He commands that you return Persephone to her Mother and the World of Light.

Hades:
Look about you, Hermes. I am absolute master of these realms. I am God of both Death and Wealth, yet my existence here in the Underworld has been a lonely one. Who can blame me for abducting the fair Persephone? I watched her often as she played among the flowers and vines of the fields. I fell in love with her then, and chose her to be my Queen; to reign with me and sit by my side as Queen of the Underworld.

She has grown weak with hunger, refusing food and drink, for to do so would insure her stay here forever. Yet you must know, Hermes, that she did finally eat the seeds of the pomegranate, and therefore cannot return to the world of the living.

Demeter (to Zeus) No! Zeus, I cannot bear to leave my daughter in the Land of the Dead! You must intervene! I will not remove my curse on the land or bless the harvest as long as she remains there! (Listens) Yes, I will accept the compromise. For the 2/3 of each year she returns to me and lives in the Land of Light, I will return my blessing to the

Earth. But when she returns to dwell with Hades as his bride, the leaves will fall from the trees and the land will be covered with ice and snow.

Persephone: Husband, though you have treated me well and I have grown fond of you, I must be reunited with my Mother and the World of Light or I shall surely perish. I shall return to you for one-third of each year, and shall then rule at your side as Queen of the Underworld.

Persephone/Demeter alternate

To the East:
Gentle Winds of the East; awaken the sleeping world to a new time and a new season. Bring forth the message of new life on the air. Kiss the seeds that lie dormant in field and forest, and tell all that it is time to bring beauty and plenty to the world once more.

To the South:
Radiant Sun of the South, increase your warmth that all life may stir with the energy of growth. Warm the world, warm the spirit, and warm the desire to live, to grow, and to bring forth a fruitful harvest.

To the West;
Blessed Waters of the West, wash the world with your cleansing, life-giving rains that nourish life once again.

To the North:
Gaia, Mother Earth, awaken every root and vine, support and sustain every branch and bough, that the world be green again and blossom and fruit spring forth in glory and abundance.

To All:
Awaken to my Magick! Awaken to the beauty of the Earth without which you would not be! Awaken to the balance of the worlds of shadow and light!

Gaia Chant : Gaia, Gaia, mother of all, creatures great and creatures small, thank you for your love and care, where 'ere I go, I find you there.

Cakes & Wine: served as usual

HPS: Each of us contain the potential for new beginnings, new life, as do these eggs upon our altar. But to fulfill the potential of promise enclosed in each egg of our desires, hopes and wishes, the eggs must be fertilized, tended and cared for. Only then can they develop and hatch, grow and mature into the realizations of our dreams.

By the Lord and Lady may these eggs be blest! And by the ancient power of the Old Ones may they be magickally charged to fulfill the promise within. An it harm none, so mote it be!

(Pass hard-boiled Easter eggs) *Line up at kitchen to peel and wash egg, return to ritual area.*

HPS: *Eat and be one with the Gods! So mote it be!*

Wine: Bless this spiritual food unto our bodies bestowing upon us health, wealth, strength, peace, and that perfect fulfillment of love, which is perfect happiness! (*Pass wine*). In this cup be the ecstasy of the spirit and the joy of the Earth. Drink and be one with the Gods!

(Pass wheel a "Wheel of the Year" person to person as the poem by Charlyn is read)

> Behold, the Wheel!
> Ever changing, never ending
> 8 portals of the year attending!
> Marking days and passing Earth time
> To honor the Lord and Lady sublime
>
> Begins the year at Hallow's Eve
> Departed ones we meet and grieve

Looking deep within our hearts
As the Sun King thus departs

Until the Yule when He returns
As light within, to flicker and burn
As we search our souls through darkest night
And seek the answers to our plight.
He strengthens and grows with Imbolg's approach
This Goddess welcomes, with no reproach.
And hope begins to lighten the land
As fertile flocks and fields are planned.

Oestara brings the promise of life,
And dreams abound to overcome strife.
We bless the creatures and the Earth
As the cycle continues of life and birth.

We honor the fairies and Otherworld creatures,
And welcome the Green Man with foliate features.
As Beltane fires burn, we salute the Spring,
The divine couple and all that they bring.

The Sun King is strong and energy high
The daylight long when Litha comes nigh.
Tend to your crops—whatever they be
And harvest the first of your fields merrily.

The burning of Lugh and the first harvest bread
Mark Lughnasadh with joy—and the Sun King with dread
As he grows weaker, the light to wane,
He gravely forsees the end of his reign.

At Mabon we give thanks for all that has been
Knowing the wheel must turn yet again.

Now light and dark even, the ageing King fades,
The fields soon lie fallow, the darkness pervades.

Constant through all, the Goddess is nigh,
Her symbol, the moon, marks the time in the sky.
Her influence guides us throughout the year,
Her love and her magick always are near.

Thank and Dismiss God/Goddess

Lord and Lady, in all your many names and all your many guises, we seek thee and honor thee. We thank you for attending our rites this night. 'Ere ye depart for your pleasant and lovely realms, we bid you stay if you will, go if you must. Hail and Farewell.

EAST:
Guardians of the East, Spirits of Air,
We thank you for giving us inspiration and knowledge,
And for your attendance to our rites this night.
'Ere ye depart for your pleasant and lovely realms,
We bid you stay if you will, go if you must, Hail and Farewell.

NORTH:
Guardians of the North, Spirits of Earth
We thank you for giving us the strength to grow,
And for your attendance to our rites this night.
'Ere ye depart for your pleasant and lovely realms,
We bid you stay if you will, go if you must, Hail and Farewell.

WEST:
Guardians of the West, Spirits of Water
We thank you for your love and understanding,
And for your attendance to our rites this night.
'Ere ye depart for your pleasant and lovely realms,
We bid you stay if you will, go if your must, Hail and Farewell.

SOUTH:

> Guardians of the South, Spirits of Fire,
> We thank you for igniting our passions and energy,
> And for your attendance to our rites this night.
> 'Ere ye depart for your pleasant and lovely realms,
> We bid you stay if you will, go if you must, Hail and Farewell.

Close circle

High Priestess (using athame or fingers) draws the circle counterclockwise from the starting place while saying (or singing) The circle is open, but unbroken, may the lord and the lady be ever in your heart. Merry meet, and merry part, and merry meet again!

BELTAIN (BELTANE)
RITUAL #1: FAIRY

Optional: outdoors May Pole dance

Needs: Stone, spear, sword and cauldron (containing cakes) at quarters, staff, CD: Fairy Heart Magic, CD: Gwydian, Songs for Old Religion, bubbles for each, fairy dust, may pole, streamers, wreath, balefire, whistle, gong, rain stick, drum

Cast Circle:

HPS: The time has come for the parting of mists. All you who would seek passage to the Otherworld, hear me! Put behind you the troubles of the mortal realm; hear the calling of the Gods, and come away. (Lead the group to the gate.)

HP: (inside gate)

Before you stands the holy gate to the Otherworld. It is the perilous bridge, the hidden cave, and the secret path. It is trod only by the wise, the heroic, and the seekers of Truth. Who hear the calling of the Sidhe?

All: We hear!

HPS: I call upon the gates of the Otherworld to open. I call upon the Mighty Ones to be present tonight, and join our circle. O Gods of my people, hear my prayer, carried by the wind on the sea.

(Water and Air enter and are smudged and aspersed, and seal the circle, then all enter, one at a time for same)

East: Winged Sylphs and fairies fair,
　　　We call thee on a breath of air.
　　　Come thou forth from places high,
　　　Wing your way through springtime sky.
　　　By the air we breathe, out and in,
　　　And by this whistle, make of tin.
　　　Come forth with sparkling fairy dust
　　　Your magick here now is a must.
　　　(blow whistle)
　　　So mote it be!

South: Salamanders and dragons wise,
　　　Rise through flame and fiery skies.
　　　Come thou forth from heat of sun,
　　　And stay until this rite is done.
　　　By the spirit fire within,
　　　And by the gong we call you in.
　　　Come ye forth with joy and light,
　　　And bring your magick here this night.
　　　(Hit gong)
　　　So mote it be!

West: Gentle Merfolk, playful sprites,
　　　From watery places to our rites.
　　　Come thou forth from oceans deep
　　　From ponds and rivers in your keep.
　　　By the blood which makes us kin,
　　　And by the rain we call you in.

Come forth with love and happy tears,
Let your magick dissolve our fears.
(Rain stick)
So mote it be!

North: Dryads, elves and gnomes of old,
From hidden realms, never told.
Come thou forth and dance with us,
Its' time for fun; now Winters done!
By the heart that beats within,
And by the drum we call you in.
Come forth; and treasures you may bring,
For magick's use within this ring.
(Drum beat)
So mote it be!

HPS: And the Tuatha de Danaans brought from those four cities their four treasures:

North: From Falias was brought the Stone of Fal, which was located in Tara. It cried out beneath every king that would take Ireland.

East: From Gorias was brought the spear which Lugh had. No battle was ever sustained against it, or against the man who held it in his hand.

South: From Findias was brought the sword of Nuada. No one ever escaped from it once it was drawn from its deadly sheath, and no one could resist it.

West: From Murias was brought the Dagda's cauldron. No company ever went away from it unsatisfied.

North: We stand upon the Stone of Destiny! *(step on flat stone)*

East: We cast the spear of Lugh Lamh-fada, *(raise spear)*

South: We draw the sword of Nuada Argat-lamh, *(draw sword)*

West: We feast with Dagda's cauldron. *(lift up cauldron)*

All: O Gods of my people, hear my prayer, carried by the wind, across the sea!

HP: It was on the first day of Beltaine, that is now called May Day, the Tuatha de Danaan came, and it was to the north-west of Connaught they landed. But the Firbolgs, the Men of the Bag, that were in Ireland before them, and that had come from the south, saw nothing but a mist, and it lying on a hill.

Ye dwellers of the south, Fomorians, Fir Bolg, monsters and tempters, and all who dwell in shadow, I lay this offering before you, that you shall be satisfied and leave our circle in peace. And on our own inner shadows let us dwell, our hatred and cowardice, our vice and falsehood, and for tonight, we cast them aside! O Gods of my people, hear my prayer, carried by the wind on the sea.

HPS: And the three things they put above all others were the plough and the sun and the hazel, so that it was said in the time to come that Ireland was divided between those three, Coll the hazel, and Cecht the plough, and Grian the sun. O Gods of my people, hear my prayer, carried by the wind on the sea.

HP: *(Thump staff three times)* The Land upholds me from below.

(Swing staff around the body three times, held vertically.) The sea surrounds me from all sides.

(Draw spiral in air with staff three times) The sky covers me from above.

I acknowledge these three realms, for such is the shape of the world. O Gods of my people, hear my prayer, for I am a wind on the sea.

HPS: And they had a well below the sea where the nine hazels of wisdom were growing—the hazels of inspiration and of the knowledge of poetry.

And their leaves and their blossoms would break out in the same hour, and would fall on the well in a shower that raised a purple wave.

And the five salmon that were waiting there would eat the nuts, and the color would come out in the red spots on their skin, and any person that would eat one of those salmon would know all wisdom and poetry.

And there were seven streams of wisdom that sprang from that well and turned back to it again; and the people of many arts have all drunk from that well.

HP: We invoke Thee, O Thou Glorious Sun,
To come Thou forth that our Will be done!
Let Thy Light illumine this Temple tonight
Making true the Magick of this Holy Rite.
(Light God candle on altar)

HPS: We invoke Thee, O Thou Soul of Night,
To come Thou forth that we may Unite!
Let Thy love work its mighty spell
A bountiful harvest to foretell.
(Light Goddess candle on altar)

HP: Queen Mab, Lady of Fairie, come to our ritual! You who are the sparkle of light on twilight's eve, You who are the flicker of green fire in the forest! Dance into our midst, Faerie Queen and join our Beltane rites! Revel with us, bring passion to our lips and joy to our hearts! Queen Mab, welcome and Blessed Be!

QM: *(CD:#1 Enters, all blow bubbles as she throws fairy dust, flirts with the men.)*

I am Queen Mab: to me 'tis given the wonders of the human
world to keep.
I am Queen of Magic, Charm and Spell
Queen of The Faeries - Wolves as well
Queen of Poets and Dreamers too
I descend from the sky to come to you
Queen of Nature and Warrior Queen
But a Queen of Mystery - Seldom seen

Queen Titania is another name
and also Maeve - we are the same
Fierce and deadly I can be
To any fool who threatens the shee
Honor me, treat my children well
And within your heart, I will dwell.
Bringing love and healing care
But don't mistreat me—don't you dare!

Pan, Lord of the wilding Night, come to our ritual!
You who are passions Lord and panic's Master!
You, who dance through the fields under the moonlight,
come hither and join our celebration.
Revel with us! Bring the Dance to our feet and Joy to our hearts.

Pan: *(Enters playing flute and flirting with the ladies)*

I am God of the forest and wood,
Who often is most misunderstood!
Protecting those who live off the land,
I'll often give them a helping hand,
Giving advice as only I could.

True, while haunting mountains, caves and streams,
I'll seduce you with your wildest dreams,
Tempt you away from your worldly pursuit,

Lure you with forbidden fruit,
Involve you in Machiavellian schemes.

The untamed forces of the night,
That startle you and cause you fright,
Are also found within your mind,
Leaving reason far behind,
Causing **Pan**-ic, fear and flight!

Yet music from my magickal pipe resounds
O're the land and through the towns
Setting toes tapping
And lovers madcapping
As life renews and the wheel turns round!

HPS: **I-O** Pan! Welcome and Blessed Be!

HP: (summon the Green Man)

Green man, come from your leafy realm,
Of Oak and Aspen, Maple and Elm,
Foliate face and coat of green
Come ye forth and be ye seen.

From the wild, from the wood
Bring thy magick green and good!
By the cup and by the wand
Rekindle now our sacred bond!

By the branch and by the vine
Enchant us all, oh Spirit Divine.
Greenman come and join our dance
And bless us with your radiance!

GM: (Green man enters, bows to Mab and approaches the altar.)

Great the rite we dance tonight
The ancient powers awake!
Moon and Sun become one light
And holy love do make…
New life we see in flower and tree
The summer comes again
Be free and fair, like earth and air
The sunlight and the rain!

HPS: Green Man, welcome and blessed be!

HP: Come! Let us erect the symbol of manhood! (Erect the maypole)

HPS: *(Bless the wreath w/pentagram)*

Blessed be this wreath of blooms,
The symbol of the divine feminine
And the gestation of the seeds and eggs which
Grow and develop into food and drink
For all living creatures

HP: *(Anoints the maypole w/holy water)*

Blessed be this phallic staff,
The symbol of the divine masculine
And the fertilization of egg and seed
Without which we would not be.

Maypole Dance: *(Pan places the wreath atop the pole. Dancers wind pole to #3- Lord of the Dance & Weavers)*

We Are Traveling In A Circle
The Circle Of The Wheel
We Are The Weavers, We Are The Woven Ones
We Are The Dreamers, We Are The Dream

Weavers (Call)
Weavers (Response)

Weavers (Call)
Weavers (Response)

We are weaving the web of life! (all)

HP: *(lights balefire)* The Balefire is lit! Let the blessings begin!

(All jump the fire, making a wish as they do so.)

Cakes & Wine: HP:

Bless this spiritual food unto our bodies, bestowing upon us health, wealth, strength, peace and that perfect fulfillment of love that is perfect happiness. (Pass cakes)

Be this bread the strength and spirit of the God, sustenance and seed of all life. Eat and be one with the Gods!

HPS: Bless this wine unto our bodies, bestowing upon us health, wealth, strength, peace, and that perfect fulfillment of love that is perfect happiness.(Pass wine)

In this cup be the ecstasy of the spirit and the joy of the Earth. Drink and be one with the Gods! (all drink)

HP: Pan, we thank you for attending our Beltane celebration this night! May your wild presence be a reminder of our connection with the natural world and of the joy within. Stay if you will, go if you must, we bid you Hail and farewell!

We give thanks also to the Fir Bolgs for leaving us in peace during our sacred celebration.

HPS: Mab, we thank you and your fair ones for attending our Beltane celebration this night! May you smile upon us from your lovely realms as the Great Wheel turns! Stay if you will, go if you must, we bid you Hail and farewell!

HP: We honor this turning of the wheel as we pass it hand to hand, speaking of our hopes for spring.

East:

> Winged Sylphs and fairies fair,
> Who came to us on breath of air.
> Who came forth from places high,
> Now return through springtime sky.
> Stay if you wish, as you are free
> Now with our thanks and blessed be,
> We say a heartfelt farewell to thee.
> Hail and Farewell!

North:

> Dryads, elves and gnomes of old,
> From hidden realms, never told.
> Who came forth to dance with us,
> And joined in our Springtime fun.
> Stay if you wish, as you are free
> Now with our thanks and blessed be,
> We say a heartfelt farewell to thee.
> Hail and Farewell!

West:

> Gentle Merfolk, playful sprites,
> Who came to enjoy our rites,
> Who came forth from oceans deep
> From ponds and rivers in your keep.
> Stay if you wish, as you are free
> Now with our thanks and blessed be,

We say a heartfelt farewell to thee.
Hail and Farewell!

South:

Salamanders and dragons wise,
Who rose through flame and fiery skies
Who came forth from heat of sun,
And stayed until our rite was done,
Stay if you wish, as you are free
Now with our thanks and blessed be,
We say a heartfelt farewell to thee.
Hail and Farewell!

Open the circle

BELTAIN (BELTANE) RITUAL #2; STREGA

Needs*: Oil lamp & everclear, 4 quarter candles & 4 extra, God/Goddess candles, stones, statue, holy water, thurible and alcohol, incense, wands, athame, 5 bells, maypole, bucket, rocks, streamers & hoop, 3 crowns, garter, Castailia Beltaine Chant & Lord of the Dance, CD player, bouquet, staff, horseshoe, capes, vials of elixir for all*

Cast and Seal circle, admit participants one at a time, sprinkle with Holy water and incense as each enters.

HPS: make gesture of Power: With your Athame in the right hand, wand in the left, raise tools and arc them down like this) (.

HPS/HP*: (Light spirit bowl saying:)*

> Awaken now, O spirit of the Old Ways,
> With your reaching blue arms
> Wake now soundly, very soundly
> We who tend the ancient fire call to you,
> Awaken Spirit Flame, Awaken!

Rite of Union*: (with hands over head)* Hail and adoration unto Thee, O Source of all Enlightenment.

(3rd eye, hands to forehead) I pray Thee impart to me thy illumination! And enlighten my mind that I may perceive more clearly, all things in which I endeavor.

(hands to solar plexus) And illuminate my soul, imparting Thy essence of purity.

(opening arms out to the side, palms up) I reveal my Inner Self to Thee and ask that all be cleansed and purified within.

HPS: *(Place athame in spirit flame, drawing power. Cast circle from the north), saying:*

In the name of Diana and Dianus, and by the Old Ones
I conjure this circle of power; become a sphere of protection;
a vessel to contain the power that shall be raised within
Therefore do I charge you and empower you. So mote it be!
     (Rap wand on the altar 3x saying) The circle is cast!

HPS:
Bautiful Diana, Goddess of the moon and beyond, think even for a moment upon we who gather in your name.

(Light Goddess candle)

HP: Dianus, God of the sun and beyond, think even for a moment upon we who gather in your name.

(Light God candle)

North: *(ring bell 3 times over bowl)*

I call out into the mist of Hidden Realms, and conjure you spirits of Earth.

Gather now at this sacred circle and grant me union with your powers.

(ring bell again 3 times, tap bowl with spirit blade 3 times)

Other quarters do the same

All Quarter people: *(come to altar, and say together)*
> I call to you, O ancient Ones!
> You who dwell beyond the Realms,
> You who once reigned in the Time before Time,
> Come! Hear the Call!
> Assist me to open the Way, give me the Power!
> Open wide the gates to the Realms of the Gods
> And come forth by these names:

North: *(face North, ring bell 3 times)* **Loudly call "TAGO"**
> *(light candle from the spirit flame and take to the North altar).*

East: *Repeat, but call "ALPENA!"*

South: *Repeat, but call "SETTRANO!"*

West: *Repeat, but call "MEANA!"*
> *(all return to their quarters w/candles)*

Statement of Purpose:

Italian Wicca is known as Strega. Diana is Queen of the Fairies, Moon Goddess, and Lady of the Lake. She was also the mother of Aradia, the later Queen of the witches. Her temple in Italy was by Lake Nemi, which in ancient times was called Diana's Mirror.

In fact, the medieval Sicilian Fairy Cult was well documented during the Spanish Inquisition. Dubbed Queen of Witches by the Christian church, the Gospels commanded total destruction of all temples of Diana, the Great Goddess worshipped by 'Asia and all the world'.

HP: I invoke thee and call upon thee Diana,
> As Queen of the Fairies,

Known also as Fauna, mother of the wild creatures,
I invoke thee by bud and stem, by leaf and flower and fruit,
I invoke thee by life and love and call upon thee
to descend into the body of this, thy Priestess and Servant.
Hear with her ears, speak with her tongue,
That thy presence may be with us this night.

(remove cloak to reveal wings, and HP places crown on her head)

HPS: Good people who walk the path of the old ways,
I come to you from the land of Tir nan og, the land of the ever living,
a place where there is never death nor transgression.
'Tis magick I bring you as the veils between the worlds are now thin,
and the time to celebrate the Lord and Lady, who wed now
in order to nourish the growing things and see them to harvest.

I invoke thee and call upon thee Dianus,
Also known as Faunus, the Horned one of Nature,
Who cares for the forest and the animals.
I invoke thee by bud and stem, by leaf and flower and fruit,
I invoke thee. By life and love I call upon thee!
Descend into the body of this, thy Priest and Servant.
Hear with his ears, speak with his tongue,
That thy presence may be with us this night.
(remove cloak, HPS places horns on his head)

HP:

Good people who walk the path of the old ways,
I come to you from the wilderness.
I protect the wild animals, the flocks and the life of the land.
I join with you now, and merry meet;
to dance and make music in honor of
the marriage of the Lord and Lady.

HPS: Between the worlds you now stand!
        'Tis a place of no-time, where magick prevails;
        a place of music and dancing; feasting and joy.
        Come, drink this elixir so that you may also see my fey companions
        and join with them in fun! (pass elixir) Drink! Join the fey!

Dancers: *Tribal Dream CD*

HPS: Ah, but alas, someone's missing I fear!
        It's the Queen of the May—she should be here!
        Who shall be queen, this lovely day?
        I'll choose her now in the old-fashioned way.
        Gather round, ladies here in the middle,
        Who'll wear the crown now is the riddle.
        (throw garter, present flowers, crown, cape,)

HP:

        Gather 'round gents and I'll throw my shoe!
        (throw horseshoe, crown, cape & staff,
        and both parade or dance to CD)
        (Optional - Could ad Faunus (Pan) here.)

HPS: (Bless the wreath w/pentagram)
        Blessed be this wreath of blooms,
        The symbol of the divine feminine
        And the gestation of the seeds and eggs which
        Grow and develop into food and drink
        For all living creatures

HP: (Anoints the maypole w/holy water)
        Blessed be this phallic staff,
        The symbol of the divine masculine
        And the fertilization of egg and seed
        Without which we would not be.

Maypole Dance: *(Faunus places the wreath atop the pole. Dancers wind pole to #1- Lord of the Dance.)*

Cakes and Wine:

HPS: *(Draw Crescent over cakes and wine)*

> Blessings upon this meal, which is as your own bodies,
> For without such sustenance, you would perish from this world.
> Blessings upon the grain, which as seed went into the earth
> where deep secrets hide.
> And there did dance with the elements,
> and spring forth as flowered plant, concealing secrets strange.

HP: When you were in the ear of grain,

Spirits of the Field came to cast their light upon you and aid you in your growth.

Thus through you shall all be touched by that same Race, and the mysteries hidden within you shall be obtained even unto the last of these grains.

(Crescent over wine) By virtue of this sacred blade,
be this wine the vital essence of the Great Goddess

(Crescent over Cakes) By virtue of this sacred blade,
be these cakes the vital essence of the Great God.

(All take a cake and wine, hold up)

HPS & HP:

> Through these cakes and by this wine,
> We Bless you, and give you inner strength and vision.
> May you come to know that within you that is of the Gods.

May this blessing be so, in the names of Diana and Dianus!
(Ring bell 3 times)

Hear us, Old Ones, we honor thee and thank thee,
Diana and Dianus Great God and Goddess of the world
before and hereafter, for your attendance.
We bid you now depart to your secret Realms.
Go if you must, stay if you will, with peace we say now: Ave, Vale!

At each Quarter: *(Ring bell 3 times)*
Hear me, Old Ones,
I honor you for your attendance and bid you now
depart to your secret realms.
Go if you must, stay if you will.
With peace we say now; Ave, Vale!
(Extinguish candle, return bowl to the altar)

HPS: *(place the blade back into the Spirit Flame)*
Sleep, Spirit of Flame,
with your reaching blue arms and red hair.
Sleep soundly, soundly, very soundly,
Until I, your friend, come again to wake you.
Sleep, Spirit of the Flame, Sleep.
(snap fingers 3 times over each element bowl and Close Circle

LITHA RITUAL: #1

Needed: God and Goddess candles, fires, incense/herbs, healing oil, bags of herbs, herbs for fire, 2 feather fans

Cast & seal circle

East: We call to the powers of the East, Realm of Wind, Land of Fairies and Sylphs. We invite you to witness this Rite and protect those who are with us.

South: We call to the powers of the South, Realm of Fire, Land of Dragons and Salamanders. We invite you to witness this Rite and protect those who are with us.

West: We call to the powers of the West, Realm of Water, Land of Merfolk and Undines. We invite you to witness this Rite and protect those who are with us.

North: We call to the powers of the North, Realm of Earth, Land of Gnomes and Elves. We invite you to witness this Rite and protect those who are with us.

HP: Gracious Lady, Queen of Night, we ask that you join us in this celebration of Mid-summer's Eve. Grace us with your love and understanding as we honor your power and presence here tonight. *(light candle)*

HPS: Great Lord, Sun King, we ask that you join us for this time of the Celtic 'Oak Festival'. Grant us your protection and care as we honor your power and presence here tonight. *(light candle)*

HP: We are standing on a threshold between worlds...at a time that is not a time, in a place that is not a place...between worlds and beyond!

HPS: Yet we are here. So it is in perfect love and in perfect trust that this circle has been cast.

Questioner: *(step forward)*

If I may...why do you call upon the Goddess and the God only by "Lady" or "Lord" and not by their names? *(step back)*

HP: Those who worship with this group come from many paths, each may be following a different tradition or pantheon.

HPS: However, when we occupy this sacred center, we are at one with the many God forms.

East: *(Step forward)* I am the Maiden, she who represents the beginning, the birth and rebirth of al things. I am the Eastern Dawn, the Spring breeze, and the Youth. You may already know me as Branwen, or to some here I am Artemis, to some Renpet, others know me as Sif, Dianna or Kore, or how many more? How many blossoms are in the field? *(step back)*

South: *(Step forward)* I am the Warrior, she who represents the fires of war and vengeance, as well as the flames of passion and desire. I am the Southern Midday, the Summer heat, and the Adult. Like my sister before me, I have many faces in many worlds. I have been called Hestia by some, Freya by others, Ishtar, Sekhmet, Inanna, Kali..all these are more... *(Step back)*

West: *(Step forward)* I am the Mother, she who represents caring and nurturing, crafts and healing. I am the Western Twilight, the Autumn rain, and the Parent. There are many names by which I have been called: Hera and Juno; Frigg, Venus and Nephthys to name a few... Persephone, Brighid, Isis – all the same heart under different faces! *(Step back)*

North: *(Step forward)* You, my children, may call me by whatever name seems befitting to your eye...old woman, grandma or Crone. I may look weak, but be careful, I have my strengths too!

I am she who represents wisdom and the mind. I am the Northern Midnight, the cold winter Earth, the Elder. Let me see...Macha? Hecate? Minerva or Gaia? Are these familiar to you? How about Cerridwen or Hel? You will come to know me in time—indeed, for time is my domain... time and the final destiny of all men, princeling or peasant... *(Step back)*

HP: There are so many names in so many paths, yet they are all aspects of the Goddess.

Questioner 2: *(Step forward)* But what of the God? I thought we were honoring the God during this Sabbat celebration...*(Step back)*

HPS: Yes, we are. In certain paths, the Sabbats are rituals for the Gods while the full moons, also called Esbats, celebrate the Goddess. This being the longest day of the year, it is only fitting to honor the Sun, which is a representation of the Lord, Great Father or the Sun King.

Holly King: *(Step forward)*

In my world, I am known as the Winter Lord, ruler of the year' dark half, whose domain is the deepest glen and the darkest cave. Those who travel the path of the Oak Men, the Druids, are like to call me Kernunnos, Wild Huntsman of the Woods, or the Green Man. And there are others...Anubis, Hades are a few, for man has always been close to the earth, yet most do seem to know of me. Today, I start to assume dominion of the Wheel, the turning of the seasons. *(Step back)*

Oak King: *(Step forward)*

I am sometimes referred to as the Oak King, the Sun, the giver of Light. You may have heard of me as Brahma or Ra, Shamas, Ormazd or possibly Ogma or Lugh. I have many faces in many paths, and as the Oak King, I reign for only one-half of the year. Though just as I am only a reflection of the Sun, so we all are but different aspects of the One. (Step back)

HP: Mid-summer's Eve is a time of great power. It is a time for healing that in your life which needs to be healed, be it physical, mental, spiritual or emotional. Both now and in the past, it is traditional at this time to pass through the smoke of the need fires.

HPS: Each one of you, in turn, should come to be anointed with healing oil, then pass between these fires. As you do so, visualize one thing that truly needs to be healed in your life. Send that energy into the fires so that they may take your desires to the gods with their smoke and flame. *(Throw herbs & incense into the fire, start CD)*

HP: As today is a day for healing, it is also a day to ask for protection. *(Bless herbs)*. These bags of herbs are for the protection of your homes. Take one and hang it over the entrance to your home.

Chant: We all come from the Sun God, and to Him we shall return as a spark of fire, rising to the heavens.

HP: *(bless the bread)* Here is a gift of the Father, made of grain and herbs which He as provided. Accept this as a symbol of our gratitude and love for you. *(place a piece in offering bowl and offer to all)*

Eat and be one with the Gods, but save a bit as an offering for otherworld entities. Toss that behind you and honor them.

HPS: *(bless the wine) Here is a gift of the Mother, made of the fruit that She has provided. Accept this as a symbol of our gratitude and love for you. (place a piece in offering bowl and offer to all)*

Drink and be one with the Gods, but save a bit as an offering for otherworld entities. Toss that behind you and honor them.

HP: Gracious Lady, Great mother of us all, we thank you for your presence and your gifts. Without your fertile presence, we would not be. Go if you must, stay if you will, we bid you 'Hail and Farewell'.

HPS: Great Lord, Loving Father of us all, we thank you for your presence and your gifts. Without your presence, we would not be. Go if you must, stay if you will, we bid you 'Hail and Farewell'.

East: Powers of the East, Realm of Wind, Land of Fairies and Sylphs, dwelling place of the Maiden, accept our love and gratitude for your presence and protection here tonight. 'Ere you return to your lovely realms, we bid you go if you must, stay if you will. Hail and Farewell.

North: Powers of the North, Realm of Earth, Land of Gnomes and Elves, dwelling place of the Warrior, accept our love and gratitude for your presence and protection here tonight. 'Ere you return to your lovely realms, we bid you go if you must, stay if you will. Hail and Farewell.

West: Powers of the West, Realm of Water, Land of Merfolk and Undines, dwelling place of the Mother, accept our love and gratitude for your presence and protection here tonight. 'Ere you return to your lovely realms, we bid you go if you must, stay if you will. Hail and Farewell.

South: Powers of the South, Realm of Fire, Land of Dragons and Salamanders, dwelling place of the Crone, accept our love and gratitude for your presence and protection here tonight. 'Ere you return to your lovely realms, we bid you go if you must, stay if you will. Hail and Farewell.

Open Circle

LITHA RITUAL #2, NATIVE AMERICAN

Needs: *quarter leathers, tobacco, corn meal, blue corn, fire pit, fatwood, sage & abalone shell, rattle, feathers, fire tokens, shells, wood tokens, eagle, coyote, salmon, bear, buffalo, dream-catchers, squares of leather/fabric, twine,*

Cast: Cast the circle with a native rattle, no words necessary

Seal Circle: Smudge with sage stick to seal

EAST Ancient and mighty ones of the East,
      Keepers of the powers of air,
      Spirits of swiftness and thought

      From the Eagle's wing we call you.
      From the stormy winds we call you.
      From beyond the clouds we call you.

      Join us this night in our sacred circle
      That our magick be witnessed
      And our sacred space guarded.
      Hiyaka!

SOUTH Ancient and mighty ones of the South
　　　　Keepers of the powers of Fire,
　　　　Spirits of passion and change

　　　　From the heart of the Coyote we call you,
　　　　From the Flame of the campfires we call you.
　　　　From the blazing sun we call you.

　　　　Join us this night in our sacred circle
　　　　That our magick be witnessed
　　　　And our sacred space guarded.
　　　　Hiyaka!

WEST Ancient and mighty ones of the West,
　　　　Keepers of the powers of Water
　　　　Spirits of love and compassion

　　　　From the mouth of the great salmon we call you
　　　　From the silver streams we call you.
　　　　From the oceans depths we call you.

　　　　Join us this night in our sacred circle
　　　　That our magick be witnessed
　　　　And our sacred space guarded.
　　　　Hiyaka!

NORTH Ancient and mighty ones of the North,
　　　　Keepers of the powers of Earth,
　　　　Spirits of strength and abundance,

　　　　From the cave of the Great Bear we call you
　　　　From the Grass and the trees we call you.
　　　　From the ancient stones we call you.

　　　　join us this night in our sacred circle
　　　　That our magick be witnessed

167

And our sacred space guarded.
Hiyaka!

Statement of intent: HP

We gather tonight to honor the turning of the Great Wheel to the season of summer. It is the time of the green earth; growing plants and growing animals. It is the time when the Sun is at its zenith and Earth feels its warmth.

HPS:
Though many of the Native people in this world have forgotten or forsaken the ways of their people, we know that they once lived in harmony with nature. All that they picked or hunted were honored. They understood that Nature gifted them the means to survive.

HP:
Their needs were simple and their hearts were devoted to their gods. In remembrance of them and the way of life they led, tonight we honor the Gods of the Pawnee people. The Great Sun who called Shakura, is currently in his full strength and glory. We come also to honor Atius Teriwa, the Great Creator, Atira, the Sacred Earth Mother, the Star People, Morning Star and Evening Star, the creators of humankind in the Pawnee tradition.

HPS:
The first tribes of people were respectful and in tune with nature and with this planet. But regretfully, many humans have turned away from the sacred in our times, even defining nature as evil, and the planet a thing to be raped, used, and abused.

HP: Atira, Earth Mother, we call thee from your Ancient and Wise realm to attend us in our ritual. Give us the wisdom to commune with the elements in accord with the Ancient ones for balance on this Planet.

Atira, Earth mother and mother of every living creature, we call to you. Be with us so that we can honor you in the old ways. Hiyaka!

HPS:

I come, for you call in sincerity. I have waited long to speak to your people, for there must be a return to the ways of old or this planet will not support life as you know it. I am the wife of AtiusTiriwa. I see you have honored me by producing my symbol, the blue painted corn for the color of the sky, adorned with white feathers to represent the clouds. Corn is the manifestation of my bounty, the life that I give to this planet in many forms as animals and plants.

It was my daughter, Uti Hiata, long ago, who taught our people how to make tools and grow food. At first, she said:

"We are hunters. You ask me to plow the ground! Shall I take a knife and tear my mother's bosom? Then when I die she will not take me to her bosom to rest. You ask me to dig for stone! Shall I dig under her skin for her bones? Then when I die I cannot enter her body to be born again.

You ask me to cut grass and make hay and sell it, and be rich like white men! But how dare I cut off my mother's hair? It is a bad law and my people cannot obey it."

But in time, she realized that the world was changing, and in order for our people to survive, she would have to adopt some of the white man's ways.

Earth:

Great Earth Mother, Atira, we honor you. Here, accept our offering of sacred tobacco as the smoke carries our prayers to you.
Hail The Earth, our Mother, without which no food could be grown and so cause the will to live to starve.
(All come forth to throw tobacco into the fire)

I shall call my husband, for I see that you are people of good heart, and will want to honor him as well. Tirawa, love, I call thee to my side. Join this celebration with great heart. Hiyaka!

HP:

I am Atius Tirawa, the Power Above; creator of the heavens and the earth. In the beginning, I called the gods together to tell of them of my plan to create the human race. Of course, I promised them a share of power for their help.

Shakura, the Sun, was assigned to provide light and heat, and Pah, the Moon, was assigned the night. I placed the Evening Star, the Mother of All Things, in the west and the Morning Star I set to guard the east.

After the gods had raised dry land from the watery chaos, I told Sun and Moon to make love, and they gave birth to a son. I then told Evening and Morning Star to make love, and they gave birth to a daughter. So the human race was made.

I taught humans to build fires, and hunt game. I taught them to speak and to make clothing of skins. I taught them to watch the stars, which would tell them when to plant, when to harvest and when to honor the Star Gods, who often descended to Earth to maintain their relationship with mortal humans.

All would have been well if Coyote had not stolen a sack of storms from Lightening for when he opened the sack, Coyote loosed the storms and so brought death into the world.

Ah, but it is Coyote's nature to bring chaos.

Hail The Great Spirit, our Father, without him no one could exist because there would be no will to live.
(all come forth to throw tobacco into the fire)

HPS:

Shakur, bright light in the sky, we come to honor you and the warmth you bring. Without you, all would perish. Grant us, we dwellers on the Earth, your fire in kindly measure. Accept our offering of wood to feed the flame, your earthly equal as we pray...

ALL: Oh, Eagle; come with wings outspread in sunny skies.
Oh, Eagle, come and bring us gentle peace.
Oh, Eagle, come and give new life to us who pray.
We remember the circle of the sky; the stars,
and the brown eagle; the great life of the Sun,
the young within the nest.
We remember the sacredness of things.

(Play Eagle Dance and do side step, each breaks away as they feel to throw stick on the fire)

HP: We are honored by your prayers, and in return, we bestow gifts upon you. *(Earth passes cloth squares)* Morning Star – first man, dawn, spring and air; what is your gift?

East: I, the Spirit of the East, offer these feathers to bring Wisdom to this tribe. May they always speak in truth. May they always remember the air!

HPS: Evening Star, bringing of sunset, gate to the spirit world, fall, and unconditional love, what gift do you bring?

West: I, the Spirit of the West, offer these shells which bring love and Compassion to this tribe. May they always be ready for the long journey. May they ever remember the Water!

HP: Great Sun, Warrior; He who shines his summer warmth upon this planet, what is your gift?

South: I am the Spirit of the South, The tokens I bring give Strength and Courage to this tribe. May they always walk the path of right living. May they always remember the Fire!

HPS: Great Star, Nights light in the Sky, what will you bestow upon the people through your gift?

North: I, the Spirit of the North, give this symbol of Earth. Let these tokens ground this tribe so that they have what they need, yet forgoing greed. May they always choose and revere the ways of nature. May they always remember the Earth!

HP: On a cold November day, one hundred and fifty years ago, the Pawnee Nation signed a treaty with the Yankton Sioux, which stands to this day. Now they fight together to protest the pollution of their sacred lands and cemeteries by the oil companies.

To remember this pact and this mission, a new symbol was created. As my gift to you, I give this symbol. May it bring you peace. May you always remember the Great Creator. *(People approach the HP)*

HPS: I, Atira, Mother Earth, too have a gift. Mine is the gift of corn, the plant that fed the Pawnee nation; the plant that represents the magick and plenty, the bounty and beauty of my green foliage, my blue sky, and my beautiful creatures. May you help to heal this planet. May you always remember the Great Mother.

(People approach the HPS)

HP: *(Cakes)* In honor of the gifts and the reverence bestowed upon all tonight, let us taste of the bounty of Earth!

HPS: *(juice)* In honor of the gifts and the reverence bestowed upon all tonight, let us taste of the bounty of Earth!

HPS: Attius Tirawa thank you for joining me here in this sacred circle tonight. It is important to meet those who follow our ways in their own way. It is good to remind them of our existence; of our ancestors, the Star People, and the need to commit to healing this planet. Go now, if you wish, or stay to feast. Hail and farewell!

HP: Atira, Great Mother, we thank you for this planet, a marvel in the universe, and for being here tonight in our sacred rites. We shall remember the lessons given us tonight and will treasure the gifts given to us. Go if you must, but stay if you will, Hail and farewell!

East:
>Ancient and mighty ones of the East,
>Keepers of the powers of air,
>Spirits of swiftness and thought
>We thank you for the gifts of your element.
>If it be your will, return now to your
>Beautiful blue realms, or stay and feast
>In good company. Hail and Farewell!

North: Ancient and mighty ones of the North,
>Keepers of the powers of Earth,
>Spirits of strength and abundance,
>We thank you for the gifts of your element.
>If it be your will, return now to your
>Earthen dwellings, or stay and feast
>In good company. Hail and Farewell!

West: Ancient and mighty ones of the West,
>Keepers of the powers of Water
>Spirits of love and compassion
>We thank you for the gifts of your element.
>If it be your will, return now to your
>Watery home, or stay and feast
>In good company. Hail and Farewell!

South: Ancient and mighty ones of the South
Keepers of the powers of Fire,
Spirits of passion and change
We thank you for the gifts of your element.
If it be your will, return now to your
Firey home, or stay and feast
In good company. Hail and Farewell!

Open Circle:

LUGHNASADH RITUAL #1:
LUGH & CERRIDWEN

Needs: *Cauldron of water and dipper, map of drought area, harvest crowns, bottles of wine and bourbon, wickerman in fire bowl, pile of wheat/grain, CD: Milling dance, dolphin dreamtime incense, burner, fan & charcoal, god & goddess candles & hurricanes, harvest décor*

Cast & seal circle:

East: Element of Air, come!
> Spring breezes blow
> Seeds sprout, plants grow
> The wheel spins as we reap and sow
> Harvest time has now begun
> Crops nourished by the sun
> So mote it be and it harm none!

South: Element of Fire, come!
> The Sun quickens the seeds we sow;
> Captured flame in the grain we grow.
> Golden fields we gratefully mow.
> Harvest time has now begun
> Crops ripened by the sun
> So mote it be and it harm none!

West: Element of Water, come!
>Living water from all sources
>Replenish the land with your life-giving forces,
>Nourish our crops, our cattle and horses.
>Harvest time has now begun
>As crops ripen in the sun
>So mote it be and it harm none!

North: Element of Earth, come!
>Fertile soil that nourishes all
>As stalks grow tall
>From seeds so small
>Harvest time has now begun
>As crops are reaped in the sun
>So mote it be and it harm none!

Statement of Purpose:

We are here to mourn the passing of the Corn God and to welcome in Lughnasadh—the harvest of grain. Without the harvest, there would be no food and without food, the people would die. His sacrifice ensures the continuation of the cycle—new seeds, new life, and the sun and rains necessary for new growth.

>Plants grow in the heat of the sun,
>Fruits ripen, bringing seeds by the ton,
>Seeds must die to be born again,
>For they must lie fallow in loam and fen.
>So must the God of Grain be zapped,
>That his vital energy is tapped!

HP: Cerredwyn, harvest Queen
>Our harvest ritual has begun
>Enter this Priestess if it be your will
>And bestow upon her your many skills
>Help us to harvest what we need

That started as idea or seed
Harming none, our will be done
So mote it be! **(place crown)**

HPS: (light candle)

I am Goddess of Fertility and Harvest,
The soul of life and the receptacle of the dead.
I am the quickening of seeds in springtime
And the glory of the ripe fields in summer.
I give the creatures of earth the gift of song,
Of the call of the drum in the dance,
And the joy of an autumn sunset.

To you I give the joy of creation
And the companion of beauty to light your days.
Fair Lugh, Shining one
Our harvest ritual has begun!
Enter the Priest if it be your will
And bestow upon him your many skills
Help us to harvest what we need
That started as idea or seed
Harming none, our will be done
So mote it be! **(place crown)**

_HP:_ (light candle)

My law is harmony with all things
Mine is the secret that opens the gates of life
And mine is the dish of salt of the earth
That is the boy and the eternal cycle of rebirth.
I give the knowledge of life everlasting
And beyond death I give the promise of renewal
I am the sacrifice, and all acts of willing sacrifice are my rituals.
I am the father of all things,
And my protection blankets the earth.

HPS: *(pass out fat wood)*
We give you fuel, that you may charge it. Let that which is past, be past. Let that which does you harm be rendered harmless. Let that which causes you to keep from you highest good be removed.

(pause until they look ready)

Add that it 'harm none', then bring forth the wood which represents those things you would have gone from your life as your personal sacrifice, and place them within the Wickerman. Give reverence to the God that He knows our honor and love.

Wickerman *(Men kneel to wickerman and say)*

Creature of corn thou art, creature of ivy and vine, now transform and become the Spirit of the Corn, the embodiment of the God who willingly goes to sacrifice that His body might sustain His people.

HP: Creature of wine, thou art, creature of grape and sugar and yeast. Now transform and become the blood of the Corn God that he will spill this day in our midst. *(Men surround wickerman, pass bottle as each ads a little wine)*

Creature of alcohol thou art, creature of corn and mash and sugar. Now transform and become the spirit of the corn, the spirit of life! *(Each man now adds a little bourbon).*

> O God of the ripening fields, Lord of the grain
> Grant us the understanding of sacrifice
> As you prepare to deliver yourself
> And journey to the lands of eternal summer.
> O Goddess of the Dark moon
> Teach us the secrets of rebirth as the Sun loses its strength
> And the nights grow cold.
> *(Burn him and sing or play "John Barleycorn")*

Milling Dance

(CD: Milling Dance. Women stand in a circle around a pile of wheat. Every other woman goes in to stamp the wheat while the rest do "step-close" moving clockwise and clapping around the pile. All exchange places. Grapevine (step side, cross other foot in front, step side, cross in back, repeat) moving widdershins (counterclockwise, women in one at a time, repeat as necessary).

Water Ritual: HPS:

Drought is again plaguing this land! The fields and forests have become tinder for any stray spark, be it from nature or man. The animals suffer and the plants and trees cry out for the nourishing rains. Let us charge and bless this cauldron of water with our plea!

> Come water, Come our way
> Bless us with your rain each day
> Quench the thirst of all in need
> Divas' please our prayer heed

(After HPS calls 'Now!' each pours a dipper of water on the map and wheat with their own request for water)

HP: Let there be desire and fear, anger and weakness, joy and peace, awe and longing within you, for these too are part of the mysteries found within you. Within me, all beginnings have endings and all endings have beginnings. I leave you now with my laughter and love. (Leaves)

HPS: Strive always for the growth of your eternal soul. Never intentionally diminish your strength, your compassion, your ties to the earth or you knowledge. I leave you now with my inspiration and my love. (Remove crown)

Cakes & Ale:

HP: *(Hold up cakes and say:)*
> Blessed be the Harvest,

Blessed be the Corn Mother
Blessed be the Grain God
For together they nourish both body and soul
Many blessings I have been given,
I count them now by this bread.

Now think of all the things you are truly grateful for! *(pause)*
Eat and be one with the Gods

HPS: *(Hold up the wine and say)*
Blessed be the Goddess of the moon, mother of all
Blessed be the Lord of the Sun, Father to everything
Blessed be the fruits of which we partake.
May our actions please you always and we harm none.
So mote it be.

East:
Element of Air
Thank you for the blessings you bestow
Bringing the spring to make seeds grow
We release you now, so you may go.
Go if you must stay if you will
Hail and Farewell.

North:
Element of Earth
Thank you for the blessings you bestow
And giving foundation so we may grow
We release you now, so you may go.
Go if you must stay if you will
Hail and Farewell.

West:
Element of Water,
Thank you for the blessings you bestow

Nurturing crops so they may grow
We release you now, so you may go.
Go if you must stay if you will
Hail and Farewell.

South:

Element of Fire,
Thank you for the blessings you bestow
The blazing sun that makes crops grow
We release you now, so you may go.
Go if you must stay if you will
Hail and Farewell.

Open Circle:

LUGHNASADH RITUAL #2

Needs: *Wine, alcohol, Celtic Circle incense, basket of herb bags, (corn dollies nearby), harvest crown, priest's shawl, loaf, CD Luna, oil*

Cast circle

Quarters come forth, 1 at a time:

Air: *(carrying incense)*
I am everywhere. I fill the fleshy pouches of your lungs; I stir all things from the smallest blade of grass to the tallest tree. I cool you with my breezes and destroy you with my storms. Without me you would die. Am I not holy and worthy of praise?

(Receives blessing from HPS then seals the circle with incense)

Fire: *(carrying flame)*
I live in the guarded embers of campfire and the pilot lights of stoves. I spring from the lightning and the hands of men. I warm you and I destroy you. Without me you would die. Am I not holy and worthy of praise?

(Receives blessing from HPS then seals the circle with fire)

Water: *(carrying bowl of holy water)*

I rise from the moist crevices of the Earth. I beat on the shores of Her body. I fall from the skies in silver sheets. Without me you would die. Am I not holy and worthy of praise?

(Receives blessing from HPS then seals the circle with water)

Earth: *(carrying bowl of earth or salt)*

I am your Mother. From me comes the fruit and grain and animals which feed you. I am your support, and my pull on your bodies keeps you held firmly to me. Without me you would die. Am I not holy and worthy of praise?

(Receives blessing from HPS then seals the circle with earth)

HPS: *'Behold, there is magick!'* or similar song.

Air:

Oh Gwydion, Prince of the Powers of Air, bring forth your breath! Lend to us your powers of magick to forge the first mighty link in this sacred circle of power! Call forth the inhabitants of your fairy worlds, and lend us your wisdom and knowledge as we open the first portal of this sacred space. So mote it be!

Fire:

Oh Bridget, Goddess of fire and beauty cast your flames around us and forge the second mighty link in this circle of power! Call forth the salamanders, creatures of fire, and bring the strength of your hearth and your knowledge and wisdom to us as we open the second portal of this sacred space. So mote it be!

Water:

Oh Mannon Mac Lir, God of the Seas, God of water, circle us with the power of your oceans and rivers and form the third mighty link in this circle of power. Call forth your merfolk to protect us and shower us with your love as we open the third portal of this sacred space! So mote it be!

Earth:

Oh Oghma, Binder, Keeper of the secrets of this earth, Ruler of knowledge and bringer of wisdom to humankind, shape this last and final link in this circle of power. Bring forth your creatures of the earth, the wee folk, and give us your heart as we open the forth portal of this sacred space and raise power within it. So mote it be!

Statement of Purpose: (2 speakers)

HP:

What will be...is. What was will be. The Wheel of the Year forever turns, dark to light; light to dark, each season passes with lessons learned.

HPS

We plant with love, tend with respect, and at Harvest time our yields reflect the bounty of our Mother Earth, ripened by our Father Sun. Yet some personal seeds we have planted, have fallen on infertile ground, or have withered for lack of nourishment. Some dreams we dreamt were not to be realized this cycle and must be relegated to the past, without regret.

HP:

Now, upon our humble hearth, gifts we offer the "Two that are One", as each day passes, shorter than the last. May we each be reminded of seasons that have passed: the seeding time, and marriage of the Goddess in May. Her womb swollen with life anew and Father Sun, is shining with so much pride through the summer months. Rising early, setting late, and now that he's supplied the warmth and light to bring to bear the Goddess and the lands, He knows that his death is drawing near.

HPS:

But this secret, he understands—that with the turning of the wheel his rebirth has been planned. Now at this time, which is not a time, in this place, which is not a place, as the God of the Grain sacrifices himself that we may be sustained, be prepared to offer your personal sacrifice as well. Prepare to sacrifice your bad habits, or the unwanted things or conditions in your life.

HP: Come to us, Mother Earth. Come to us and take your ease. You have labored long and hard to bring forth your bounty so that we, your children, may survive. Come! Relax, for well have you earned your rest. Eat and drink your fill. Sing, dance, and be merry, for you have done well, and there is plenty for all. We shout your praises, for you are the essence of fulfillment, love and joy. May we never forget that we are a part of your Sacred Body, and may we work to preserve it in all of its myriad forms. All hail Great Mother, Danu! Hearth Mother, Earth Mother, please be our guest tonight!

(places harvest crown on Priestess)

HPS:
Come to us, Lord of the Hunt, Sacred Herdsman and Divine Smith. Put by your horn, lay aside you crook, stow your hammer and quit your forge for now. Wipe your brow and come find your leisure in the midst of our good company. Have a seat, put up your feet, and pour yourself a cold drought. By the virtue of your work have you earned a rest, for well have you cared for the wild beasts and domesticated flocks. And many a time has your forge burned long into the night with you hard at work creating lightning bolts of such exquisite beauty and terrible power as we have ever beheld. Join us, Great Lugh, and indulge yourself to the fullest. May you know no want in our presence, for thanks to you and the Goddess, we know no want. We raise our voices high to your greatness. All hail the God of the Wild Magicks.

Listen to the words of the Great Father, who of old was call Osiris, Adonis, Zeus, Thor, Pan, Cernunnos, Herne, Lugh, and by many other names.

HP:

I, who am the Lord of the Hunt and the Power of the Light, sun among the clouds and the secret of the flame, I call upon your bodies to arise and come unto me. For I am the flesh of the earth and all its' beings. Through me all things must die and with me are reborn. Let my worship be in the body that sings, for behold all acts of willing sacrifice are my rituals. Let there be desire and fear, anger and weakness, joy and peace, awe and longing within you. For these, too, are part of the mysteries found within yourself. Within me, all beginnings have ending and all ending have beginnings. So mote it be. Hear now the words of the Mother.

HPS:

I, who am the beauty of the green earth and the white moon upon the mysteries of the waters, I call upon your soul to arise and come unto me for I am the soul of nature that gives life to the universe. From me all things proceed and unto me they must return. Let my worship be in the heart that rejoices, for behold, all acts of love and pleasure are my rituals. Let there be beauty and strength, power and compassion, honor and humility, mirth and reverence within you. And you who seek to know me, know that the seeking and yearning will avail you not, unless you know the mystery; for if that which you seek you find not within yourself, you will never find it without. For behold, I have been with you from the beginning and I am that which is attained at the end of desire.

Milling Dance –

Sacrifice:

We are here to mourn the passing of the Lord of the Grain and to welcome Lughnasadh, the season of Harvest. Without the harvest there would be no food, and without food, the people would die.

Take these blessed packets of herbs and make them your personal sacrifice. Charge them with that you would be rid of—a bad habit, a negative emotion, an unhappy condition…always adding the protective words, 'an it harm none'. Once charged, place them in the wickerman to burn your sacrifice with his.

(When they are done, make pentagram sign to wickerman and say)

Creature of corn and wood, ivy and vine, now transform and become the Spirit of the grain, the embodiment of the God who willingly goes to sacrifice, that His body might sustain His people!

HP: *(Hold up chalice of wine)* Creature of wine, thou art! Creature of grape and sugar and yeast, now transform and become the blood of the God that he will spill this day in our midst. *(Pour it on wickerman)*

HPS: *(Hold up chalice of booze)* Creature of alcohol thou art; creature of grain and mash and sugar. Now transform and become the spirit of the grain, the spirit of life! *(Pour on wickerman)*

From the Goddess you came and to the Goddess you shall return. Lord of the Grain we have come for your body! (Lights wickerman)

Chant:
> *We all come from the Goddess*
> *We all come from the Sun God*
>
> *And to him we shall return*
> *Like a drop of rain, flowing to the ocean.*

HP: (when burned, say:)
Fire cleanses and purifies! The spirit of the Grain has been set free!

Loaf

The seeds have been planted, have grown in the hot sun, matured, and now are harvested. Grain becomes flour, and flour becomes bread. Bread—merely flour, water, yeast and salt—as the world is merely earth, water, fire, and air.

These four elemental ingredients—grain from the fields, water from rivers and mountain streams, leavening from the wild yeasts of the air, and salt from the sea, have been combined for thousands of years to sustain the children of the earth.

Cakes & Wine:

HPS;
Thus do I strengthen my Lord! His energy resides in this bread, a record of all life that ever was and all that is yet to come. So mote it be! (Go to each who tears off a piece)

May you never hunger! Eat and be one with the Gods!

HP: Thus do I bless the fruits of which we partake! The energy of the Goddess resides in this wine, a record of all life that ever was and all that is yet ot come. So mote it be! (pass cups)

May you never thirst! Drink and be one with the Gods!

The wheel turns as we step into the months of autumn. As the nights grow longer and the darkness reaches over the land, we secure the abundance of the harvest against the barren months to come. With every meal in the waning season, remember the spirits that gave their lives so that we might live. Bless and revere them. Blessed Be.

HP: Mighty Goddess Danu, Earth and Hearth Mother, we thank you for your presence tonight. Your loving guidance is always with us. Stay if ye will, go if ye must. Hail and Farewell!

HPS: Lugh, God of Light and the Arts, your light fills our hearts with life and gladness. We thank you for your presence tonight. Stay if ye will, go if ye must. Hail and Farewell!

East: Gwydion, Sweet Prince of Air, return now, if you must, to the brisk autumn breezes which are brimming with the excitement of the year's climax. Take with you our gratitude for your presence in our sacred circle this night. But stay if you will, and join us in feast and celebration. We bid you Hail and Farewell.

North: Oghma, Keeper of the Secrets of the Earth, return now, if you must, to the Earth where worms burrow deeper and seeds nestle awaiting the long sleep of winter. Take with you our gratitude for your presence in our sacred circle this night. But stay if you will, and join us in feast and celebration. We bid you Hail and Farewell.

West: Great Mannon Mac Lir, God of Water and the Sea, return now, if you must, to the autumn rains which cool Earth's fevered brow, baked in the heat of summer afternoons. Take with you our gratitude for your presence in our sacred circle this night. But stay if you will, and join us in feast and celebration. We bid you Hail and Farewell.

South: Fair Bridget, Goddess of fire and beauty, return now, if you must, to the dying fires of autumn's heat soon to give way to winter's chill. Take with you our gratitude for your presence in our sacred circle this night. But stay if you will, and join us in feast and celebration. We bid you Hail and Farewell.

Close Circle

MABON RITUAL #1- APPLES

Needs: *Gold altar cloth, harvest decorations, gold & silver candles, basket of apple tokens, apples for altars, quarters & libation, apple cider, incense & charcoal, craft sticks, fire bowl & wood, lighters, CD*

Cast & seal circle

East: Spirits of the East, element Air,
> Summer breezes yield now to autumn chill.
> Energy wanes and thoughts grow still
> To seek within and give thanks for all
> That has matured with the coming of fall.
> Beauty surrounds us in colorful hue
> Autumn trees and skies of blue.
> Come Fairies, join our sacred rite
> And dance with us in joy tonight.

South:
> Spirits of the South, element Fire,
> Summer heat yields to cool days ahead
> Light wanes for the God is dead.
> His sacrifice will bring life anew
> And for this act we bid thank you.
> Fires dance still in our hearths' and hearts
> Till your northward journey starts

Come Dragons, join our sacred rite
And dance with us in joy tonight.

West:

Spirits of the West, element Water,
Autumn rains wash the empty fields
Bountiful the harvest yields.
Soon your rain will turn to snow
And ice impedes the river's flow.
Help us find what we now seek
Sustain us through the winter bleak.
Come Merfolk, join our sacred rite
And dance with us in joy tonight.

North:

Spirits of the North, element Earth
Abundant fields have given their worth
Soon to rest through winter deep
As seeds and trees go now to sleep.
Guide us to our spiritual best
Impart your magick to our quest
Come Gnomes, join our sacred rite
And dance with us in joy tonight.

Statement of Purpose:

Leaves fall, the days grow colder. The Goddess pulls the mantle of the Earth around Her as the Great Sun God sails toward the West—to the lands of Eternal Enchantment. Fruits ripen, seeds drop, and the hours of day and night are balanced. Yet soon the dark will outlast the light and chill winds will blow in wailing lament.

In this seeming extinction of nature's power, we know that life continues; for spring is impossible without the harvest as surely as life is impossible without death.

Tonight we celebrate Thanksgiving, honoring the sacrifices that have been made by field and flock. We also come to give thanks for the fruits we have harvested in our lives.

HPS: Sun King, Corn King, God of the Harvest, your seed has provided a bounty that has greened the meadows and filled the fields. As the burning embers of summer are overtaken by darkness and you begin your descent to the Underworld, we ask that you bestow your blessings on this sacred circle. Come to us one last time as Consort of the Queen.

HP: I am the stag of seven tines
      I am a flood on a plain
      I am a wind on the sea
      I am a tear of the sun
      I am a hawk upon the cliff
      I am the cunning navigator
      I am the power of transformation

      I am a giant with a sharp sword, hewing down an army

      I am a salmon in the river
      I am the skilled artist
      I am the fierce boar
      I am the roaring of the winter
      I return again and again like the receding wave

Great Mother Goddess, Brigid, Demeter, Queen of the Harvest, your body has provided abundance and beauty. As you begin your metamorphosis into Crone, bless us with your wisdom. Come to us and join your Consort one last time.

HPS: I am the womb of all that lives.
      I am the blaze on every hill.
      I am the queen of every hive.

I am the shield to every head.
I am the tomb to every hope.

Who but myself knows where the sun shall set?
Who foretells the ages of the moon?
Who brings the cattle from the house of Lir?
Who shapes weapons from hill to hill?
wave to wave, letter to letter, point to point?
Who but myself?

HP:

This world passes from summer into the dark of the year. On this day of the Equinox, this day of balance, we pause on the threshold where light begins to fade.

As the nights grow longer it is time to reflect on your life and cultivate inner wisdom. It is of great importance that you leave all negative thoughts and emotions behind as you enter the New Year.

Place all disappointments, grief, self-doubt, pain and fear gathered during this turning of the wheel into this wooden stick. When you feel you have done this, burn it in the fires of transformation.

CD? *I am the fire*

HPS:

One sacred harvest fruit has been celebrated throughout time as one with special magick—the apple. When an apple is cut in half across the middle, (Cut apple) it reveals a star, the symbol of the goddess, her womb and her promise of immortality. Five is the sacred number of the Goddess for it represents the five elements; air, fire, water, earth and Spirit.

The pentacle is the orbit described by the planet Venus, the Morning & Evening Star which heralds the rising of the sun and which shines even after the sun has set; a promise of its rebirth.

HP:

The apple resembles the sun, which is born anew each dawn, then travels across the sky, changing color from yellow to red as it sets in the western sky. It journeys through the underworld to be reborn in the rosy dawn in a froth of apple blossom clouds. Thus the apple represents happiness and youth in the afterlife, and the resurgence of life after death.

I call to Kore!

Kore: (carrying apple)

I am Kore, Maiden of Spring but may be best known as Persephone, Queen of the Underworld. The apple is my symbol. I was abducted by Hades, King of the Underworld and carried to his domain to rule by his side. Only after my mother Demeter withdrew he powers of fertility from the Earth did Zeus agree to free me—but only for part of the year. It is time now, for me to return to the land of shades, and while I am there, Demeter will withdraw her powers and the land will lie fallow until I return in the spring.

HPS: I call to Pomona, Keeper of the Orchards and the fruit trees.

Pomona

I am Pomona. Wood Nymph am I—she who causes the trees to flourish, bloom and bear fruit. You may have heard of my marriage to lusty Vertumnus. I had many suitors, but Vertumnus disguised himself as an old woman who convinced me that Vertumnus was the right husband for me! Through our union we two are responsible for the apple tree's prolific nature. Thus, the apple has become a symbol of love in many lands.

HP: I call to Morgan!

Morgan:
Behold, I am the Triple Mother Goddess and Fairy Queen. I am Priestess of the Old Ways over the sisterhood of nine who inhabit the mystical Isle known as Avalon.

Avalon is a refuge for the spirits of the dead, but also a place of magick and healing, for here at the very center of the isle stands the fabled apple tree whose magickal fruit promises immortality.

HPS: I call to Idunn!

Idunn:
I am the keeper of the Golden Apples. Each day, I carefully open the casket in which they are kept and give one to each of the Gods to eat. This magickal fruit keeps them young and beautiful, which is of paramount importance to them, being of mixed ancestry, both God and mortal.

Once Thiassi, a storm giant, was so desirous of possessing me and my Golden Apples that, with the aid of Loki, he kidnapped me! **Never** did I give Thiassi a taste of my precious apples!

Deprived of my youth-giving apples, the Gods in Asgard began to fade and age. Loki was forced to rescue me.

This basket contains magickal apples inscribed with a message for you from the Gods. Select one, read and contemplate it. Determine how it applies to your life and your soul's growth. (pass apples)

HPS:
It is equally important to give thanks for those good and wonderful things that have come to you through this turning of the Sacred Wheel of the year. Think now, upon these things, and send your gratitude to the Lord and Lady.

Chant & spiral dance ;

> Queen everlasting, Mother of all
> We thank you for the coming of fall
> We thank you for the coming of fall
>
> Mature crops sustain our needs
> And provide for next year's seeds
> And provide for next year's seeds
>
> For earth's bounty now revealed
> We give thanks for the harvest yield
> We give thanks for the harvest yield

Cakes & ale:

HP: Bless this fruit of the harvest that has given its life that we might live. Sow, plant, reap. This is the cycle of the earth. This is the never-ending cycle of life.

Eat and be one with the Gods!

HPS: Bless this juice of the sacred apple, this reminder of the cycle of seasons and the cycles of our lives and symbol of the wisdom and healing power of the Goddess.

Drink and be one with the Gods!

HP:

> The Horned One returns to the belly of the Mother.
> Warrior of Light, go to your rest and dream of rebirth.
> Great God of Grain, we send our last wishes with you
> That you rest and prosper in Summerland.
> God of Night, as you take your throne in the West,
> look with benevolence upon your children
> and grant us the hidden knowledge of our true wills.
> Stay if you will, go if you must, we bid you hail and farewell.

HPS: The Great Goddess transforms into the powerful Crone.

Mighty Mother of All, as you enter your most powerful aspect of Crone and cast the veil of night over your head in preparation for winter, look with kindness upon us, your children and help us to grow in strength and joy. Guide us through the coming dark. Great Mother, we ask that you favor us with your wisdom. Stay if you will, go if you must, we bid you hail and farewell.

East: Spirits of the East, element Air,
> We thank thee for thy gentle breeze
> And even for the winds that freeze
> For without them we would not be
> The breath of life you guarantee.
> We've given thanks for the beauty of fall
> These lessons given we will recall.
> Return to beauteous planes where you dwell
> Stay or go if you must, Hail and farewell.

North: Spirits of the North, element Earth
> We thank thee for thy bounty reaped
> Grain and squash and pumpkins heaped
> For without the harvest we would not be
> To sustain life, you are the key.
> We've given thanks for all that's good
> And mysteries deep we've understood.
> Return to beauteous planes where you dwell
> Stay or go if you must, Hail and farewell.

West: Spirits of the West, element Water,
> We thank thee for the rain and snow
> As toward the winter time we go.
> For without them we would not be
> That life goes on, you guarantee.
> We've given thanks for all your gifts

And for your presence as the season shifts.
Return to beauteous planes where you dwell
Stay or go if you must, Hail and farewell.

South: Spirits of the South, element Fire,
We thank thee for your warming glow
Essential for all things to grow.
For without this, we would not be
We've given thanks for our hearts desire.
And to our greater good aspire.
Return to beauteous planes where you dwell
Stay or go if you must, Hail and farewell.

HPS:

As the two become one, we follow them into darkness. The seasons change, the Wheel of the Year turns, and we shift into the dark times. With gratitude for the good things past, we turn our personal journey inward. Blessed Be!

Open circle

MABON RITUAL #2- LORD'S DEATH

Needs: Apples, apple cider, oil lamp, rock, chalice, censor, popsicle sticks for all written on before ritual, bowl of petals/herbs, sun/moon tokens, staff, oak crown, circlet, CD & player.

Cast & seal circle

East: Guardians of the watchtowers of the East,
        I summon, stir and call thee!
        Come, gentle winds whose briskness now is felt
        Come whisper in the golden leaves
        And gently kiss the ripening fruit
        For we stand on the threshold of the darkness,
        As summer breezes give way to autumn chill,
        So mote it be!

South: Guardians of the watchtowers of the South,
        I summon, stir and call thee!
        Come heat of the sun to warm our days still
        As the sun moves further and fire fades,
        to be replaced with the chill of the night.
        Come forth wise ones, ancient gods,
        And keep us safe during winter's plight.
        So mote it be!

West: Guardians of the watchtowers of the West,
I summon, stir and call thee!
Come gentle rain, not yet turned to snow,
Come as we reflect on the guidance of the gods,
and let the cool autumn rains cleanse us,
Purifying our hearts and our souls.
And preparing us for our spiritual quest.
So mote it be!

North: Guardians of the watchtowers of the North,
I summon, stir and call thee!
Come, robed in yellow and rust and green,
Come bringing forth the bounty of the Earth,
As the world passes from light into darkness,
and the golden fields of the earth bring the promise
of food and nourishment through the winter.
So mote it be!

HPS: Goddess of the field and god of the hunt,
All power of the elements are yours.
I hereby declare created this Mabon Circle.
By the power invested in me in another time
And another place, I declare this circle sealed.

HP: Statement of Purpose

At this observance of the final equinox of the ending year, our awareness shifts to the coming dormancy of Mother Earth. But even as the year begins to die, in the falling of leaves and the frosted, flowered death of gardened rows, we gather here in affirmation of the love that engenders life, reproducing the fertile seed of birth and seasonal renewal.

HPS: Let us consecrate according to ancient custom the Return of Balance between Light and Dark.

East: (raising censor) Light.

West: *(raising chalice)* Dark.

East: Air.

West: Water.

East: East.

West: West

HPS: *(knocks with staff in middle of Circle)* I am the Reconciler between them.

South: (raising Lamp) *Heat.*

North: (raising Salt) *Cold.*

South: *Fire.*

North: *Earth.*

South: *South.*

North: *North.*

HPS: (knocks with staff) I am the Reconciler between them.

East: *Creator.*

North: *Preserver.*

West: *Destroyer.*

South: *Redeemer.*

HPS: One Reconciler between them. *(Knocks with staff).*

Brief is the balance but for an instant between the Lord of Light and the Lady of Shadows. At this equinox of the ending year, the waning Sun must bow before the dark-kindled Lord of Shadows.

Veiled in cloud-cloaked, misty mantles, the final, flickering beams of Midsummer warmth linger, yet cool and give way to the retreating rays of Summer's dying Lord.

HP: Oh Silvered Lady, Queen of the Shadowed Seasons,
    I call to thee!
    Come into this, the body of thy Priestess
    That we may know and honor thee. *(place circlet)*

HPS: I am the Silvered Lady of the Shadowed Seasons,
    But am known of old by a myriad of names
    And a multitude of faces: Anna, Perenna, Pomona, Ceres,
    Demeter, and Habondia.
    Welcome the wonders of my weather-witcheries,
    I fling scattered flakes of first frost
    Upon ripened fields ready for reaping;
    The harbingers of colder climes to come.
    Welcome the magick of my spoken spells;
    As I whisper vesperal incantations,
    Invoking purple-woven vapors
    Into twilight tapestries of early Autumn evenings.
    Lord and consort, Oak King, I call to thee!
    Come into this, the body of thy Priest
    That we may know and honor thee!
    (Place oak crown)

HP: I am the fire within your heart,
    The yearning of your soul.
    I am the Hunter of Knowledge
    And the Seeker of the holy Quest.

I, who stand in the darkness of light,
Am He whom you have called Death.
I, the Consort and Mate of Her we adore,
Call forth to thee.
Heed my call beloved ones,
Come unto me and learn the secrets of death and peace.
I am the corn at harvest
And the fruits of the trees.

I am he who leads you home,
Scorge and Flame,
Blade and Blood
These are mine and gifts to thee.

Call unto me in the forest wild
And on hilltop bare
And seek me in the Darkness Bright,
I who have been called Pan, Herne, Osiris and Hades,

Speak to thee in thy search.
Come dance and sing
Come live and smile,
For behold; This is my worship.

You are my children and I am thy Father.
On swift night wings
It is I who lay you at the Mother's feet.
To be reborn and to return again.

Thou who thinks to seek me,
Know that I am the untamed wind,
The fury of the storm and passion in your soul
Seek me with pride and humility,

But seek me best with love and strength.
For this is my path,
And I love not the weak and fearful.
Hear my call on long Winter nights

And we shall stand together guarding Her Earth
As She sleeps.

(HP falters, a chair and cloak is brought and he whispers to HPS)

HPS: My Lord soon makes his sacrifice. He has asked one thing of you. You have sown and reaped the fruits of your actions, good and bane. Now must you banishing all misery and hate, and find the courage to plant seeds of joy and love in the coming year. ***Place your fears, your failures, your guilt, resentment or disappointments in the fire as your sacrifice.*** *(All put sticks in fire, CD; Circle of Seasons #8.)*

HP   As the days grow colder, and the nights last longer,
       May I remember the summer past.
       With sunlight fading, and hearth inviting,
       My memories will warm my soul.

       From a season of hard work and hard play,
       I hear Mother's voice calling me forward.
       While I rest, She shall lull me with songs of a dream,
       As close to Her bosom I cling. (he dies)

HPS: The wild god has gone to rest in the Underworld, retuning this night to the belly of the Mother. Let us remember his former glory, Light enthroned in celestial shafts of gold, traversing the sky in summer strength, coaxing the growth of meadowed pastures and fertile fields. Sol Invictus! We remember the glory that was Thine,

Tonight I become the Crone, my most powerful stage. I am the wise one, the giver of life and the one who calls home all that have reached the end of life. The deepest of mysteries are mine, and I bid you seek within to discover the truth in yourself and in my teachings. Remember that even though winter is coming, the light will return again and take comfort!

Therefore, in joy, give thanks to the Great Mother of Harvest Home and to the departed Sun King, the Horned Consort of the Lady, Pan of the Sacred Pipes, Maddened Dionysius of the Holy Vine:

Lady and Lord. Come forth and speak of your thankfulness and remember the blessings of yet another year, fast receding into the mists of memory.

(All offer herbs to the fire, give thanks then receive a token, spiral dance to CD Castalia Hidden, Circles #5.)

HPS:

The apple is sacred and magickal fruit; a symbol of the gods for it holds the knowledge of the ancients inside. Tonight we ask the gods to bless us with their wisdom. Drink now the juice of this sacred fruit and be thankful.

(*Cut apple and hold up*) Five points in a star, hidden inside stand for earth, air, fire, water and spirit. Tonight we ask the golds to bless us with their bounty. Eat now of this sacred fruit and be thankful.

HPS:

My Departed Lord, we shall take comfort in the memory of Thy radiance! Hallowed Blaze of Heaven and the manifest splendor of the Sacred, Thou hast been the living Light, source of inspiration to sage and saint, Priestess and prophet. We bid thee good rest. Hail and farewell. (*Remove circlet*)

Goddess of this gilded season, transforming foliage from green to gold and preparing the dying year for its resting place in the bosom of Winter's embrace; We graciously thank thee and acknowledge the

Mystery of Thy Presence in every falling leaf. We ask Thy guidance through this season of lengthening shadows, while we remember with thankfulness the abundance of Thy harvest bounties which hast been given us. We bid thee hail and farewell!

East: Guardians of the watchtowers of the East,
  And all good creatures of fairy and wing,
  Accept our gratitude for your presence here,
  And know that you may remain with us
  As we feast of the bounty of the Mother
  Blessed Be.

North: Guardians of the watchtowers of the North,
  And all good creatures of earth, fauna and foliage,
  Accept our gratitude for your presence here,
  And know that you may remain with us
  As we feast of the bounty of the Mother
  Blessed Be.

West: Guardians of the watchtowers of the West,
  And all good creatures of spirit and waters,
  Accept our gratitude for your presence here,
  And know that you may remain with us
  As we feast of the bounty of the Mother
  Blessed Be.

South: Guardians of the watchtowers of the South,
  And all good creatures of fire and strength,
  Accept our gratitude for your presence here,
  And know that you may remain with us
  As we feast of the bounty of the Mother
  Blessed Be.

Open Circle and feast!

Printed in the United States
by Baker & Taylor Publisher Services